72-78072

4/21/73

Chinese Mystics

CHINESE MYSTICS

Edited and with an Introduction by

Raymond Van Over

HARPER & ROW, PUBLISHERS
New York, Evanston,
San Francisco, London

I would like to thank C.C. Chambers for expert editorial assistance and S.D.G. without whom nothing could have been accomplished.

For permission to quote from the following selections, the editor makes grateful acknowledgment to the following publishers and authors:

Taoist Teachings, the Writing of Lieh Tzu, translated by Lionel Giles, John Murray (Publishers) Ltd.; "On Trust in the Heart," translated by Arthur Waley, from *Buddhist Texts Through the Ages,* ed. by Edward Conze, Bruno Cassirer (Publishers) Ltd.; *The Platform Sutra of the Sixth Patriarch,* translated by Philip Yampolsky, Columbia University Press.

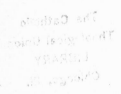

CHINESE MYSTICS. *Copyright © 1973 by Raymond Van Over. All rights reserved. Printed in the United States of America. For information address Harper & Row, Publishers, Inc., 10 East 53rd Street, New York, N.Y. 10022. Published simultaneously in Canada by Fitzhenry & Whiteside Limited, Toronto.*

FIRST EDITION

STANDARD BOOK NUMBER: 06-066821-0

LIBRARY OF CONGRESS CATALOG CARD NUMBER: 72-78072

Designed by Ann Scrimgeour

Contents

Introduction

The great fundamental concepts of Chinese philosophy, religion, and culture were present in remote antiquity—and even then were considered ancient. As in most early cultures they did not exist as separate entities, but shared the recognition of a unifying spirit that animated all life. Distinctions were blurred, boundaries between objects, people, and animals were permeable. Animals often possessed divine attributes; and divine beings, spirits, and even legendary figures were all part of a system that saw life as an extremely intimate, interrelated, and interdependent force.

A deep and abiding love of nature is evident throughout the earliest religious and philosophical writings of the Chinese. Their abundant ancient literature is full of the beauty of crystal streams, placid lakes, and sharp angulated mountains that so dominated the landscape that their earliest religious symbolism developed around nature themes— mountain, wind, trees, fire, heaven. In this early literature we can see a world slowly humanizing, but retaining its original primordial knowledge of natural forces at work. This was a world where the night sky was not a distant or strange place but an extension of animal and earth; where a blessing was bestowed upon those who could sense best the knowledge of *Hsuan P'in* (the animal-goddess), and *Ti* (the earth-goddess); who could identify the ways of nature as early man dwelt in the mists of a fertile earth that contained a vital spirit in every bird, stone, or murmur of spring rain. Such insights inevitably must have led to an appreciation of the *mysterium tremendum et fascinosum* for a transcendent divinity that underlay the complexity of nature's forms.

In later times the system became a somewhat corrupted form of Taoism and geomancers appeared who interpreted the *feng shui,* or "influences of wind and water," much as divination from wind and animal entrails developed in the West. Hence, some estimate nature worship in China developed into a "natural philosophy" as early as 4000 B.C.

Arnold Toynbee, the noted English historian, has expressed the central relationship between man, nature, and worship as intimate and irreducible. "These elements of Nature-worship embedded in living higher religions are something more than the fossilized remains of a dead primitive religion; they are indications that, below the surface of the psyche, the worship of Nature is still alive. It is alive because the Non-Human Nature over which Man won his decisive victory in the Upper Palaeolithic Age is only one half—and this is the less. formidable half—of the Nature with which Man is confronted. The other half of Nature, with which Man still has to cope, is Nature as he finds her within himself."[1]

The inspired writers of the *Bible* understood the archaic beauty of primal nature as did the Taoist priest-poets. The *Bible* expresses this inspired language of God as "the groaning and travailing of creation," a summation of the child's explusion from the womb as well as the tumultuous straining of a virgin mountain cracking up through the skin of the earth, or even of a spring pressing quietly but persistently into expression.

Pantheism seems a natural religion for men with such a clear animistic insight, for it is in the primitive world that all the beauty and terribleness of an overpowering and fateful force is made manifest. The theological and philosophical criticism of pantheism as a religion, even in the so-called "higher" religions, is that the creator is reduced to the level

[1] *An Historian's Approach to Religion* (London & New York: Oxford University Press, 1956), p. 22.

of the created, and thus equated with mundane affairs. In effect, transcendency is denied to the Godhead. God, therefore, it is argued, disappears into the stream of life and natural processes. But is this so? It has been said that mystics, the greatest advocates of pantheism in the higher religions, "want to dissolve the world in God."[2] But the weakness of this argument is that it views the mystic wrongly, as in a mirror—the primitive pantheist did not see God as lost or dissolved in nature, but nature dissolved in God. And the religious mystic of the higher religions (as opposed to the "primitive") sees nature both dissolved in God, and God dissolved in nature—resulting in a blended aesthetic, a unity of all things in God—and God in all things.

Unlike early Judaism and Christianity, Chinese nature worship did not take on the aspect of a God-rejected religion, but was incorporated into elaborate pantheistic rituals —eventually surfacing as simply a natural force, or dynamic, that existed in all living things, including humankind. In their earliest religious books one finds constant emphasis on a natural force or life-energy (*Ch'i*). In this way people were never divorced from the power of nature, or even of God, for identification with the rhythms of life meant partaking of it to the Chinese. As all life continued effortlessly, coming from no spring and moving to no ocean, so could mankind drink of immortality. For the seasonal destructions were observed to be never final. The tree that lost its greening luster, that appeared dead and gray during winter, was resurrected in the spring. And so all life was a manifest of this dynamic rhythm. The ancient Chinese believed that a man seeking salvation had simply to shed the self-imposed delusions of his character and stand in the stream of life. The Chinese philosophers believed that they thereby became masters of their own condition and partners of their gods.

It is no stranger to observe the primitive pantheist altering

[2]See L.H. Grunebaum, *Philosophy for Modern Man*, Preface by Ernest Nagel (New York: Horizon Press, 1970), p. 319.

his limited concepts of animism and polytheism to the unitive and universal enlightenment of the Chinese mystic, than it is to observe that the character of God (Jehova) alters from a tribal deity in the early pages of the *Old Testament* to the universal Godhead of the mature Jewish and Christian churches. But no matter how theologians and religious writers have tried to escape it, pantheistic concepts continually develop when discussing mysticism. That is because there is a justifiable connection, and even as orthodox a figure as Thomas Aquinas explains creation as *emanatio totius entis ab uno*, or, emanation of all that is from One. But Aquinas goes even further and "maintains that God is in all things, potentially, essentially, and present."[3] Such thoughts would of course be damned as pantheistic by many theologians, as would sympathetic passages in the *New Testament* where God is seen as the "All in All."

A similarity of such pantheistic expression can be found in many Western saints, but one of the most dramatic examples is St. Francis's intimate relationship with nature and his passionate love and involvement with all natural life. In a language Hermann Hesse describes as "eternally human," St. Francis called all creation his dear brothers and sisters. Even when he was faced with a red-hot iron that doctors had ordered to sear his forehead, he greeted the smoldering iron as his "dear brother, the fire."

The Taoist sage Chuang Tzu wrote: "The heavens and the earth and I have come into existence together, and all creation and I are one." This supreme reality Chuang Tzu speaks of is the Tao, and is the foundation upon which all Chinese mystical religion and philosophy was built. All the schools of Chinese thought can be said to have held the concepts of Tao in common, for all the old deities were their common origin.

The ancient Chinese also recognized the close relationship between the poetic function and the exalted life. Arthur

---

[3]F. Max Muller, *Theosophy or Psychological Religion* (London: Longmans, Green, and Co., 1893), p. 514.

Waley has pointed out that Chuang Tzu's method of communicating the Taoist "no-knowledge" was essentially that of the poet.[4] The capacity of poetry to excite religious feelings in regard to both people and nature was used by the Chinese mystics not only to communicate what we in the West consider basically ineffable; they also developed it into a technique for exciting the awareness that stimulated the "ineffable" religious experience.

Perhaps after all is written and argued about the ineffability and the "characteristics" of mystical experience it would be best to approach the writings of mystics as one would a religious poet. The poetic reference is not out of place regarding Chinese mysticism. The essence of Taoist thinking can be seen in the poet's conception of his craft. Robert Frost, for instance, felt that poetry is—that which is lost in translation. A more Taoist idea cannot be expressed!

The Tao in its utter neutrality means simply "Way"—not even "*the* Way"—which would imply directionality or exclusivity. And it is this concept of Tao, which has been rendered in the West as equivalent to the vague concept of "natural law," that is at the heart of all Chinese religious thought. But, and this is often forgotten, Confucius also incorporated Tao into his teachings. Most people popularly consider Confucius a strictly ethical and social philosopher. But the basis of Confucian philosophy can be seen as the ethical aspect of Tao, the Way of man rather than the metaphysical Tao or an abstract law drawn from nature. The Confucian concept of *Ju,* which was a humanist, personalist, and ethical doctrine, differs from the Tao in its emphasis, but retains the premise of finding the *Reality* of life through the action or non-action of man in relation to the world around him. The Taoist teaches that the "superior man"[5] finds his ultimate reality in the center of "self." But this

---

[4]"Preface," *Three Ways of Thought in Ancient China* (New York: Doubleday and Co.), 1956.

[5]For a further discussion of the Confucian "superior man" in relation to the *I Ching,* see the introduction to a new version, edited by Raymond Van Over (New York: Mentor Books, 1971).

cannot be obtained except through placing oneself in harmony with "Heaven" or the rhythms of the universe.

Lao Tzu spoke of, and Taoism came to mean, an acceptance of the spiritual oneness of all that exists, of action without assertion, and of a natural man instead of a conditioned, striving man seeking illusory, unnecessary goals. Quiet and peace within the soul would be accomplished, Lao Tzu taught, by a natural honesty rather than an educated shrewdness, of non-interference with the rhythms of life and rather a joining, a union with all nature. Such a philosophy lies at the heart of all pantheist and mystical religions, and extols the mystic's essential belief in the soul of living things in direct communion with a universal reality.

The classical Chinese philosophers–mystics continually emphasized the basic premise which underlies all early Chinese thought (especially Taoist)—the idea of Nature as a dynamic spiritual principle, and man's relationship with natural order as the foundation of his salvation. The sublime order of the Universe and Nature, of both *T'ien* (Heaven) and *Ti* (Earth), can be clearly found in early Chinese writings, especially in the *I Ching* or *Book of Changes*, the *Tao Teh Ching*, the *Chung Yung*, and the other ancient classics.

Nature was seen as an extension of universal order, and if man was to be happy and find his true self, he must conform to the "ways of Heaven." As E. R. Hughes points out in his introduction to *Chinese Philosophy in Classical Times*,[6] "the remarkable thing is that whilst the idea of T'ien was less and less permeated with the idea of personality, it was through this reverence for sublime Nature that human personality was recognized as indispensable for the good life of man in society. Man must obey; but in order to be able to obey he must be free, free to be his true self." This idea of freedom to be his true self was a subtle and constant influence in both Chinese political and religious philosophy. But the violent, changing feudal system under which China

[6]London: J. M. Dent & Sons Ltd., 1966.

existed from even before the time of Christ, made political enlightenment difficult; while in religious philosophy, which was also subject to numerous pressures and changes, the idea of self-discovery played a constant role—far more central than in Western religious philosophy. And when Buddhism was introduced at the latter part of the Han period (206 B.C.–A.D.220), this natural tendency for self-exploration of the Chinese was enhanced. Intense speculation about the nature of the Self is central to Buddhist philosophy and can be seen in many Buddhist writings (represented in this anthology by the *Surangama Sutra*, and the *Sutra of 42 Sections*), or the writings of the great ninth-century Indian philosopher-mystic Sankara—as well as in Western mystics like Meister Eckhart. In both the Eastern and Western approaches to this central question about the nature of man, a common agreement exists—that to grasp and eventually become one with that "Real Self" it is necessary to recognize its "other world" aspect. In Buddhism it is the *Anyad*, the "wholly other." Sankara writes of achieving this level of Being as another realm entirely: "He who has reached the all-penetrating Atman" enters into the All. Eckhart writes of this *alienum* from the empirical Being and movement to the "wholly other" attribute of Being as a unifying sense of the All as well: "He becomes all things," says Eckhart. In Taoism, this is seen as the Way, which is both immanent and transcendent. It is a nameless reality that emanates everywhere. Purgation and Self-knowledge are implied by Lao Tzu, who writes:

> The secret waits for the insight
> Of eyes unclouded by longing;
> Those who are bound by desire
> See only the outward container.

The Tao signifies the Way in which the universe evolved, the Way man and the world functions. "It is wisdom to know others," says Lao Tzu, but "It is enlightenment to know one's Self."

The Characteristics of
Mystical Experience East and West

Mysticism has always been a mystery to the greater number of people. To the popular mind it has come to mean magic, occultism, or any strange or esoteric phenomena—especially those reported from the East. These are all grave misuses of the term. Its original Greek meaning did indeed relate to "those who are initiated into the Eleusian mysteries," but its truest meaning cannot be separated from a religious aspiration common to all cultures East and West. A mystic is best defined (in general terms) as one who practices putting himself into direct relation with Deity or other unifying principles of life. This is necessarily broad, and while mystics vary within the framework of different religions, there seems a great deal of similarity between the language and experiences of mystics the world over.

After a careful psychological and philosophical analysis of mysticism, W. T. Stace lists seven basic characteristics common to all cultures, religions, periods, and social conditions.[7] His conclusions are drawn from Christian, Islamic, Jewish, Mahayana Buddhist (a major influence on Chinese Ch'an Buddhism and Japanese Zen), and Hindu texts. Stace breaks down the mystical experience into two basic psychological types: the extrovertive and the introvertive. It may be instructive to compare his findings with those developed by D.T. Suzuki, a renowned Buddhist mystic and modern interpreter of Zen (Ch'an) Buddhism for the West.[8] In an

[7]It would be extremely helpful for the interested reader to study Stace's chapter on this subject: "The Problem of the Universal Core," Chapter 2, *Mysticism and Philosophy* (London: Macmillan & Co., 1961).

[8]Comparisons between Stace's and Suzuki's categories are sometimes impossible to make—for the subtleties of language, the complexities of experiences, and the various cultural differences make the task overwhelming. Stace properly dedicated a complete book to the task of analyzing parallels between East and West, but I have gone ahead with the listing and parallels because they are still very instructive for initial understanding of mystical experiences.

introduction, it is not possible to detail completely the characteristics of mystical experiences and these lists and commentary should serve only as a rough guide.

EXTROVERTIVE	INTROVERTIVE
1. The unifying vision, expressed abstractly by the formula "All is One." The One is, in extrovertive mysticism, perceived through the physical senses, in or through the multiplicity of objects.	1. The Unitary Consciousness, from which all the multiplicity of sensuous or conceptual or other empirical content has been excluded, so that there remains only a void and empty unity. This is the one basic, essential, nuclear characteristic, from which most of the others inevitably follow.
2. The more concrete apprehension of the One as being an inner subjectivity of all things, described variously as life, or consciousness, or a living presence. The discovery that nothing is "really" dead.	2. Being nonspatial and nontemporal. This of course follows from the nuclear characteristic just listed.
3. Sense of objectivity or reality.	3. Sense of objectivity or reality.
4. Feelings of blessedness, joy, happiness, satisfaction, etc.	4. Feelings of blessedness, joy, happiness, satisfaction, etc.
5. Feeling that what is apprehended is holy, sacred, or divine. This is the quality which gives rise to the interpretation of the experience as being an experience of "God." It is the specifically religious element in the experience. It is closely intertwined with, but not identical with, the previously listed	5. Feeling that what is apprehended is holy, sacred, or divine. (Perhaps it should be added that this feeling seems less strong in Buddhist mystics than in others, though it is not wholly absent and appears at least in the form of deep reverence for an enlightenment which is regarded as supremely

characteristic of blessedness and joy.	noble. No doubt this is what explains the "atheistic" character of the Hinayana Buddhism. It should be noted that the feeling of the definitely "divine" is as strongly developed in the pantheistic Hindu mysticism as in the theistic mysticisms of the West and Near East.)
6. Paradoxicality.	6. Paradoxicality.
7. Alleged by mystics to be ineffable, incapable of being described in words, etc.	7. Alleged by mystics to be ineffable.

In his second series of essays on Zen,[9] D.T.Suzuki lists the "chief characteristics of satori":

> 1. *Irrationality.* By this I mean that satori is not a conclusion to be reached by reasoning, and defies all intellectual determination. Those who have experienced it are always at a loss to explain it coherently or logically. . . . The satori experience is thus always characterized by irrationality, inexplicability, and incommunicability.

Stace's characteristics 6 and 7 may be compared with Suzuki's description here. But an important difference in temperament is that with their finely developed sense of the paradoxical Chinese mystics would not even attempt a clear or rational explanation of this experience—in contrast to Western mystics who, as Rudolf Otto has pointed out, have habitually tried to explain it even while accepting it as ineffable.[10]

> 2. *Intuitive insight.* There is a poetic quality in mystic experiences and this applies also to the Zen experience known as satori. . . . The knowledge contained in satori is concerned with

[9]*Essays, Second Series* (Boston: Beacon Press, 1952), pp. 28–34.
[10]Rudolf Otto, *The Idea of the Holy,* (London: Penguin Books, 1959), p. 16.

something universal and at the same time with the individual aspect of existence.

Satori is a Japanese term, equivalent in Chinese to *wu*, which means "eternal non-being" according to Lao Tzu. It is the first principle of Tao, and is opposed to material objects. Wu literally means "not," and is generally associated with *wei*, which means "action"—the combination *wu-wei* being a central and important Taoist *and* Buddhist concept of non-action, or actionless activity. Another major Taoist idea associated with wu is *wu-hsin*, which means literally no-mind, a state achieved by the same spontaneous, non-choice, non-discriminatory "mind" as practiced in wu-wei. Both of these descriptions and their philosophical modifications were developed by the fifth-century philosopher Tao-sheng, who also initiated the important Ch'an principle of "sudden enlightenment."[11]

In most introvertive mystical experience, when consciousness is dissolved from its dependence upon the physical senses, and emptied of all "empirical content," the mind becomes what is described as a "void" as pure consciousness emerges. But how then does "consciousness" perceive or gain knowledge? All direct links with the senses are gone and *noesis*, or a direct intuitive experience, becomes the foundation of knowledge and all "knowing." Noetic understanding presents special difficulties, for while agreeing with Christian mystics in their description of the Absolute as "Nothing," the Taoist and Buddhist have a specific approach to knowledge, reason, and "knowing" the Absolute.

In Japanese, satori is defined (by the Buddhist scholar Christmas Humphries) as "A technical term used in Zen

---

[11]For a more complete description of this peculiarly Chinese Buddhist point of view and the philosophy of Tao-sheng, see Fung Yu-lan, *A Short History of Chinese Philosophy*, (New York, London: Collier-Macmillan Free Press, 1948), pp. 249 ff. See also Chapter 1 where Fung Yu-lan discusses important differences between the religion and philosophy of both Taoism and Buddhism.

Buddhism to describe a state of consciousness beyond the plane of discrimination and differentiation." But this direct knowledge or intuition (noesis) is not simply abstract knowledge. Basic intuition is "the profound unity which is identified as the real self." All forms of Chinese mysticism seek "enlightenment" by resolving the distinctions between subject-object opposition. As this occurs the "real self" (and unity) is made manifest. But how then does one achieve this identification with the real self, and thereby directly perceive the Way?

Rational argument or reason is not unknown to the Chinese sage, but with the Taoist (or the Ch'an Buddhist who carried on the tradition), "spontaneity" is highly valued. This concept played a prominent role in Taoistic thinking from its beginning and will be found throughout the writings in this anthology. Spontaneity—*tzu-jan*, literally meaning "being so of itself"—is more than simply action without thought, for it is conceived of as a dictum of nature and of the natural process. This central concept of Taoism is seen as discarding knowledge, ceasing to make distinctions and imposing one's own will on nature, but rather seeking to recover the spontaneity of a child, and allowing actions to respond "of itself." Water is a popular analogy in Taoism to express the natural spontaneity of life. It is ceaseless but unconcerned activity: "I follow the Way of the water instead of imposing a course of my own . . . I do it without knowing how I do it. . . ." writes Lieh Tzu.

This tzu-jan is not a blind or inattentive reaction in the sense of English "spontaneity," but rather spontaneity through complete identification with the world around one. If a person is *en rapport* as it were, with his surroundings, spontaneity is a natural reaction. If not, it is forced and based on discrimination. Taoists believe that the "Way" was lost when reason discriminated between one's Self and the world about one. To return to the Way is to stop discriminating *(pien)* and perceive (noesis) Nature itself—not its forms. But how does one return to the Way when the primary admonition is to "do nothing" (wu-wei)? Non-action in order to accomplish something is obviously paradoxical—and it is precisely what the Taoist means. The Tao does not mean idleness, or "doing nothing" in the Western sense of that phrase. Wu-wei is one of the main themes of the *Tao Teh Ching* and remains central to all Chinese mystical writings. In the *Tao Teh Ching* it means following along the line of least resistance, as water follows a dry riverbed in the spring, until any resistance tires and ceases all together. (Judo, for instance, is founded on this purely Taoist principle.) In such an effortless way, the gentler principle overcomes the more active, harder principle. Water overcomes and wears down even the hardest rock. For this reason rational discourse is incapable of defining the Tao. How can one define the wearing away of rock by water? "The Way that can be told is not the constant Way." In such a slow process knowledge is worn away until direct perception of "knowing" is achieved. This can only be accomplished by great and long discipline, not by un-thinking indulgence or idleness. The purpose of all this "non-activity" to achieve "enlightenment" is described by A.C. Graham in his *The Book of Lieh Tzu* as: "return from motion to stillness, from existence to the Void, the Nothing out of which all things emerge and to which they go back in endlessly recurring cycles."[12]

> 3. *Authoritativeness.* By this I mean that the knowledge realized by satori is final, that no amount of logical argument can refute it. Being direct and personal it is sufficient unto itself. . . . Satori is thus a form of perception, an inner perception, which takes place in the most interior part of consciousness. . . . Zen perception being the last term of experience cannot be denied by outsiders who have no such experience.

[12]London: John Murray, 1960, p. 5.

Compare this to Stace's characteristic 3, where he lists a sense of conviction that goes beyond normal perception, that is more real than reality. That the experience is also "direct and personal" parallels it with Stace's number 7, for it takes place on such a profound inner level that words fail.

> 4. *Affirmation.* What is authoritative and final can never be negative. . . . Though the satori experience is sometimes expressed in negative terms, it is essentially an affirmative attitude toward all things that exist. . . . it accepts them as they come along regardless of their moral values. . . . Buddhists call this "patience," or more properly "acceptance," that is, acceptance of things in their suprarelative or transcendental aspect where no dualism of whatever sort avails.

This description of *total* involvement and interrelatedness of everything can be applied to most of the Western mystics' experiences. "To talk about mind or nature is defiling," Suzuki warns. "All is Zen (Ch'an) just as it is, and right here you are to apply yourself. Zen is suchness—a grand affirmation." Even pantheism places a wrong emphasis in Suzuki's thinking, for it implies a dualism of nature and God, or at its closest to Ch'an concepts, phenomenal nature is seen as a garment of God. But even here the dualism is too strong for the Chinese mystic and must be left behind.

> 5. *Sense of the Beyond.* Terminology may differ in different religions, and in satori there is always what we may call a sense of the Beyond; the experience indeed is my own but I feel it to be rooted elsewhere. The individual shell in which my personality is so solidly encased explodes at the moment of satori. . . . My individuality, which I found rigidly held together and definitely kept separate from other individual existences . . . melts away into something indescribable, something which is of quite a different order from what I am accustomed to. The feeling that follows is that of a complete release or a complete rest—the feeling that one has arrived finally at the destination.

This feeling, which Ch'an followers describe as "coming home and quietly resting," can be related to numbers 2 and 5 of Stace's categories. It is perhaps parallel to what early

Greek philosophers, like Heraclitus and Anaxagoras, talked of when they extolled the "sense of the boundless" in human nature. Heraclitus in particular felt that human nature "had no boundaries" and those that we did suffer were created in lieu of fuller understanding. In apprehending what the Western mystic would call sacred or holy, there is the same loss of the individual personality and the complete obliteration of the objective world. This is more common to Eastern mystics, whereas in the West it is spoken of as a process of "union" or "transformation" into a new being. Although finding the Tao, or returning to whence we came as Taoists would put it, cannot take place without transformation, or what in Christianity is called *metanoia*, a change of heart. But this identification with God, and man becoming "unified," is again not what Ch'an sages mean when they say satori—for the dualism is still too strong—but other forms of Eastern mysticism, such as certain aspects of Taoism and Buddhism, would not find it difficult to identify with the Western description.

> 6. *Impersonal Tone.* Perhaps the most remarkable aspect of Zen (Ch'an) experience is that it has no personal note in it as is observable in Christian mystic experiences. There is no reference whatever in Buddhist satori to . . . Father, God, the Son of God, God's child, etc. . . . We may say that all these terms are interpretations based on a definite system of thought and really have nothing to do with the experience itself. At any rate, alike in India, China, and Japan, satori has remained thoroughly impersonal, or rather highly intellectual.

As Suzuki observes, this is *the* unique difference between Eastern and Western mysticism. Stace does not incorporate any personal divine elements in his categories either, but the testimony of many Western mystics reveals a great amount of sensual and personal commentary relating to the experience. This impersonal quality applies to all the Chinese mystical tradition except the lowest, most corrupt form of Taoism where deities, sub-deities abound. Taoism in its corrupt form, for instance, gave birth to the belief that·

thirty-six thousand gods resided in the human body and had
to be dealt with through the magic of a Taoist priest-magi-
cian whenever illness struck. But this type of Taoism does
not apply to the higher forms of Chinese mysticism.

> 7. *Feeling of Exaltation.* That this feeling inevitably accompa-
> nies satori is due to the fact that it is the breaking up of the
> restriction imposed on one as an individual being, and this
> breaking up is not a mere negative incident but quite a positive
> one frought with significance because it means an infinite ex-
> pansion of the individual. . . . But the Zen feeling of exaltation
> is rather a quiet feeling of self-contentment; it is not at all
> demonstrative, when the first glow of it passes away.

This most clearly relates to Stace's category 4 of blessed-
ness and joy. The Western mystics—far more than the
Eastern—are subject to emotional ecstasy. Unlike the Christian mystic who often conceives of the soul as longing like
a lover for return to God and achieve union (in Western
occult and alchemical lore this is expressed as the *coniunctio*
or *Chemical Wedding*), and who seeks the Divine Ground
passionately and even evoking sensuous language as the only
effective parallel to mundane experience, the Chinese mystic is convinced of the single, unitive, Divine substance
which permeates all things and thus is satisfied with a disci-
plined and rigorous uncovering of the Divine within himself.

The raptures and the sensuous poetry of the Western mystic are lacking in Chinese mystics. He suffers no passionate
longings for God, nor does he wait for death to deliver his
soul to the Deity after a lifetime of devotion and love.
Buddhism in particular does not speak of an objective Deity
the soul should seek or attempt to unite with. If one speaks
of Deity at all in Buddhism it is in terms of the individual
awakened soul, the individual Self enlightened through conscious awareness of its true and eternal nature. And while
the Christian concept of Deity makes God an objective
force—and often anthropomorphic to a disturbing degree—
even Judaism, which also objectifies the Deity as a majestic

and powerful Being, would not speak of longing passion, of love and union with Jehova. This would have been considered in bad taste or an insult to their concept of God. Indeed, Jewish mystics consider it "not lawful" or improper and indecorous for one to give any accounting at all of his mystical experience. Such experiences, contrary to Christian tradition, were usually kept secret and imparted to a few chosen disciples.[13]

In the early mythological religions there is also little passionate union between the human and divine. Mythological deities occasionally succumbed, and human and divine relationships occurred, but these were rare and the immortal gods were kept clearly beyond the range of the sort of unification Christian mystics spoke about. Even from the earliest writings it can be found that the Chinese tended to see the human and divine as single and of one source. There is the Chinese inscription from the Valley of the Orkon, written around A.D. 133, that began with the words: "O Heaven so blue! there is nothing that is not sheltered by Thee. Heaven and men are united together, and the universe is one (homogenous)." In the more practical sense, the Chinese tendency to harmonize, as they had from the beginning between heaven, nature, and man, can be seen in their syncretic approach to the three major religions of Confucianism, Taoism, and Buddhism living "side by side" in daily life (notwithstanding a number of major religious purges through the ages).

> 8. *Momentariness.* Satori comes upon one abruptly and is a momentary experience. In fact, if it is not abrupt and momentary, it is not satori. . . . This abrupt experience of satori, then, opens up in one moment an altogether new vista, and the whole existence is appraised from quite a new angle.

Most people think of mystics and mysticism generally as strictly introvertive. But Stace has tried to show otherwise.

[13]See. G. G. Scholem, *Major Trends in Jewish Mysticism* (New York: Schocken Books, 1967), p. 21.

He believes extrovertive experience is characterized by being sensuous and consists in a transfiguration of actual sense perception, whereas an introvertive experience is formless and void of any type of imagery or sensuality.

The abrupt quality Suzuki spoke of in his eighth point compares with the extrovertive experience which comes upon one suddenly and spontaneously. While the extrovertive experience may occur again, the individual has no power to bring it back or make it end. The introvertive experience, on the other hand, is achieved by special techniques of internalizing one's attention—which differ according to various cultures and traditions.

While the extrovertive achieves union by utilizing his senses and is acutely aware of the multiplicity of the phenomenal world mystically transfigured, his ultimate perception is the resolution of this multiplicity—the chair, the house, the tree, the mountain, the sky, all become fused into a Unity that permeates them all. The introvertive achieves the same experience by consciously and willfully shutting down his senses, by slowly and painstakingly dissolving awareness of the multiplicity of impressions that float into his mind. Thus he plunges into his own inner depths—and thereby unites with what the Buddhists call the Real Self; again, in this darkness and absolute quiet a sense of unity is achieved, devoid of any plurality at all.

Once achieved, the "acquired" introvertive experience can often be induced at will and sometimes retained over long periods of time—so the individual is in effect living in what the Christian church would call a "state of grace." The introvertive experience is, however, usually intermittent and of brief duration which gives rise to periods of depression and aridity as the individual suffers an acute sense of loss or darkness—what St. John of the Cross beautifully calls the "dark night of the soul." And even within the introvertive or acquired tradition, there are few who achieve a lasting or even permanent mystical consciousness running concurrently with normal consciousness. This peculiar condition of intermingling states where the exalted and mundane states of consciousness are fused is very rare. But some, such as St. Teresa and Ruysbroeck, achieve what has been called the Illuminative Life. St. Teresa, it is reported, went about her considerable day-to-day administrative duties while in a mystical ecstasy—it being sustained even while performing such mundane tasks as scrubbing the floor. St. John indicated that "the soul has it in its power to abandon itself, whenever it wills, to this sweet sleep of love."

The dichotomy between the sudden and gradual attainment also exists in Vedanta. If Nirvana is obtained stage by stage and one obtains the sought-after blissful union with Brahman, and then on to the true knowledge of the Self, or Atman, it is called *Kramamukti*, or gradual liberation. If this same enlightenment is obtained "in the twinkling of an eye" during one's lifetime, it is called *Givanmukti*, or life-liberation, and is equivalent to the sudden enlightenment of Japanese, Chinese, and Christian mystics.

A similar developement into two schools—the sudden and the gradual—took place in Zen, the Japanese counterpart to the fusing of Taoist mysticism and Ch'an Buddhism. While the Japanese Soto school emphasizes gradualness in attaining satori, the Rinzai school stresses its sudden and abrupt nature. D. T. Suzuki writes of the Rinzai approach: when satori comes, it is "a bolt of lightning. The flight from the alone to the alone is not, and cannot be, a gradual process."[14]

With the exception of the personal, sensual, emotional element in Christian and Sufi mysticism, all of these characteristics of the mystical experience can be found, one degree or another, in the Chinese religious tradition represented in this book. As the Chinese philosopher Fung Yu-lan describes it, "In order to be one with the Great One, the sage has to transcend and forget the distinctions between

[14]D. T. Suzuki, *Essays in Zen Buddhism*, First Series (New York: Grove Press, 1961), p. 215.

things." It is the drive and capacity for unity, for the giving of one's Self up to the "Great One," that describes the mystic's final goal. He seeks, with total abandon and dedication, to unite himself with the Godhead.

The variations found in the dogma of individual expressions of this experience do not change its fundamental nature. R. F. C. Zaehner, for instance, attempted a strictly Christian interpretation of this *unio mystica* and compares non-Christian mysticism unfavorably with the Christian experience. But arguing over the shape of a canister does not change its contents. True, there are important differences between the world's leading religions and the references to that fact are scholarly and long. But the similarity of superficial facts—such as Eckhart and Ruysbroeck experiencing a Godhead beyond the trinity just as Brahman lies beyond the Hindu Brahma, Vishnu, and Shiva—are not the only foundation upon which a perennial philosophy rests. It is the testimony of the experience itself. For whether it is called Godhead by Eckhart, or Brahman, Nirvana, Samadhi, Wu, Satori, Sunyata, does not alter the basic similarities or the experience's impact upon the human spirit and personality.

Editor's Notes on the Selections

The writings included in this anthology represent the heart of early Chinese religious and philosphical spirit. Selections were made for *The Chinese Mystics* with the idea of introducing the reader to the essence of Chinese mystical religous thinking. Individual religious philophers and thinkers were always evaluated with that idea in mind, as well as for their style, content, and individual contribution to Chinese culture and philosophy. The parallels with Western religious and mystical practices in the introduction and footnotes are therefore tenuous.

D. T. Suzuki has argued that "Zen is neither psychology nor philosophy." And Rudolf Otto, in his introduction to Ohasama's book *Zen*, argues against confusing the magical, oriental world with Western philosophical ones. Because I agree with these assessments, the emphasis on Western parallels in this book and the footnotes have been almost exclusively with Western mystical and religious writings—the only valid parallel for oriental mysticism. For the obscurity of *Ch'an* anecdotes, of magical terminology, *koans*, and *kwatsu*, and concepts such as *satori, nirvana*, and *wu*, are all intimately a part of the *mysterium ineffabile* of the world's mystical tradition. In reading Chinese mystical literature, one often gets the impression of touching the heart of a secret, of sighting as through a mist the spirit of China —only to find oneself rudely pulled up short by the unexpected. In Western mystical writings there is frequently an attempt at the poetic or rational. The grotesque and absurd is often either suppressed or translated into occult lore, whereas in Chinese writings the whole human condition is laid bare, with paradox and absurdity gladly accepted.

The ideas, analogies, metaphors, and language, as well as the philosophy and religious experience contained in these writings are unquestionably the strangest on earth. Taoism,

Buddhism, Ch'an Buddhism, and the early classics represent a sophisticated and arcane tradition. Of these, the writings of Lieh Tzu and Chuang Tzu are probably the best introductions into such strange terrain. But I have listed the classical early writings first not only because of their natural place in time, but because the *Tao Teh Ching* should be the first writing in the book that the reader comes upon. For it is the concept of the Tao, the path all things move upon, that is common to all of China's philosophical and mystical schools. The Chinese mind expressed in these writings is arcane and mysterious not because the thoughts themselves are beyond the grasp of a Westerner, for the ideas dealt with by Chinese mystics are part of the human spirit, not separate from it. The difficulty arises from the unique Chinese syntax, and in the development in Chinese culture of certain key phrases that best express their own profound understanding of the human condition. It is this uniquely Chinese "way of thinking" that demands careful and intense consideration. James Legge, one of the greatest turn-of-the-century translators, expressed his feelings that "In the study of a Chinese classical work (or any Chinese writing), there is not so much as interpretation of the characters employed by the writer as a participation of his thoughts—there is the seeing of mind to mind." It is for this reason that I recommend approaching Chinese mystical writing initially as poetry and secondly as religious revelation or philosophy.

The Early Classics

The three selections included in this section of the book have been called "The Three Mystical Scriptures" by the Wei-Chin Mystical School philosophers. They are the foundation for most of the later Chinese mystical writings.

The *I Amplification*, or *The Great Treatise* as it is sometimes called, is one of the most important "wings" or books of the *I Ching*. The peculiarly Chinese concept of *I*, or change, is not mentioned in the first two wings of the *I Ching*'s text. And it is not until we come to the fifth and sixth wings that the *I* concept is developed. In these two wings alone, which comprise *The Great Treatise*, the character for *I* is mentioned fifty times. While explaining much of what is found in the text of the *I Ching*, *The Great Treatise*—which is more Taoist than Confucian even though his name is associated with its construction and meaning—concentrates on the origins of the *Pa Kau* or eight trigrams, the methods pursued in the practice of divination and the development of Chinese arts and culture.

There are several great figures in Taoism. In the earliest period is the legendary figure of Lao Tzu, whose book the *Tao Teh Ching* remains the heart of Chinese mysticism. Other early figures are Lieh Tzu and Chuang Tzu, who brilliantly championed Lao Tzu's vision of the Tao. This is not a proper place to get into the argument about the muddled origins of these books. The Lieh Tzu writings, in particular, have been brought into question—particularly by scholars such as William Theodore de Bary, Wing-Tsit Chan, and Burton Watson—where it has been pointed out that they may well be the product of a Neo-Taoist writer of the third century A.D. instead of the misty character Lieh Tzu. His pedigree does not interest us here. And neither does any argument over which chapter of the Chuang Tzu is actually by Chuang Tzu or later Taoist writers. The writings of these men that have been selected for this anthology stand as a valuable introduction to early Taoist writings. The brilliant character and wit of Chuang Tzu is intact, as is the gentle persuasion of the Lieh Tzu writings. It has been said, and with some justification, that Taoism cannot be understood without the aid of Chuang Tzu and Lieh Tzu. For that reason, while the whole eighty-one chapters of the *Tao Teh Ching* have been included, an even greater number of pages have been given over to the writings of Chuang Tzu and Lieh Tzu.

Another Taoist writer included is Huai-nan Tzu (d.122 B.C.), the last great Taoist philospher of the early period before the Neo-Taoism of the third and fourth centuries A.D.

The history of Ch'an Buddhism in China is long and complex, and selections were included because of the profound Buddhist influence upon Chinese mystical philosophy and religion.[1] Two points only need be made here. The Ch'an school was radically different from orthodox Buddhism and its most radical departure was initiated by Hui-neng, the Sixth Patriarch, who is represented in this anthology by selections from his *Platform Sutra*. This is considered one of the most important influences in both Chinese Ch'an and Japanese Zen beliefs. Some consider it one of the great classics of Ch'an-Zen literature. Hui-neng's rise is important because of his strong emphasis on sudden enlightenment, and iconoclastic attitude toward the traditional ritual, Buddhas, and Bodhisattvas.

The Sutra of 42 Sections was included in its entirety because of its central and important position in Chinese Buddhist literature. It contains many characteristic Buddhist thoughts and is believed to be the first Buddhist literature introduced into China from India. *The Surangama Sutra* was also included as one of the earliest Buddhist statements to have a deep impact on China.

Because of the great amount of Chinese religious and mystical literature, the economics of publishing, and the natural bounds of space, numerous writings and selections were omitted. I would have liked to include a number of selections from Huang Po and *The Transmission of the Lamp*, the *Chung Yung*, the mystical writers of the Wei-Chin School (in particular Wang Pi), Sheng Chao, selections from the Diamond and Lotus Sutras, and many others. I can only hope that the selections that were made will stimulate further reading into what is a complex, subtle, and fascinating subject.

[1]The reader is advised to turn to the excellent *Buddhism in China, a Historical Survey* by Kenneth Ch'en for a complete history (Princeton, N. J.: Princeton University Press, 1964).

Chinese Mystics

Part 1
CLASSICS/
EARLY
WRITINGS

Tao Teh Ching
The Book of Lao Tzu

CHAPTER 1
Embodying The Tao

The Tao that can be trodden is not the enduring and unchanging Tao. The name that can be named is not the
enduring and unchanging name.

(Conceived of as) having no name, it is the Originator of
heaven and earth; (conceived of as) having a name, it is the
Mother of all things.

> Always without desire we must be found,
> If its deep mystery we would sound;
> But if desire always within us be,
> Its outer fringe is all that we shall see.

Under these two aspects, it is really the same; but as
development takes place, it receives the different names.
Together we call them the Mystery.[1] Where the Mystery
is the deepest is the gate of all that is subtle and wonderful.

CHAPTER 2
Nourishment of the Person

All in the world know the beauty of the beautiful, and in
doing this they have (the idea of) what ugliness is; they all
know the skill of the skillful, and in doing this they have (the
idea of) what the want of skill is.

---

[1]This word, *Hsüan*, is a close equivalent of "mystic" or "mysticism."
Taoism is also known as the *Hsüanchiao*, or the "Mystical Religion" of
China. This first chapter sets forth immediately the kernel of Taoism. To
understand the Tao one must partake of its nature. The parallel with
Western mysticism is clear—both emphasize the necessity of *experiencing*
the "cosmic mystery."

So it is that existence and non-existence give birth the one to (the idea of) the other; that difficulty and ease produce the one (the idea of) the other; that length and shortness fashion out the one the figure of the other; that (the ideas of) height and lowness arise from the contrast of the one with the other; that the musical notes and tones become harmonious through the relation of one with another; and that being before and behind give the idea of one following another.

Therefore the sage manages affairs without doing anything, and conveys his instructions without the use of speech.

CHAPTER 3
Keeping People at Rest

Not to value and employ men of superior ability is the way to keep the people from rivalry among themselves; not to prize articles which are difficult to procure is the way to keep them from becoming thieves; not to show them what is likely to excite their desires is the way to keep their minds from disorder.

Therefore the sage, in the exercise of his government, empties their minds, fills their bellies, weakens their wills, and strengthens their bones.

He constantly (tries to) keep them without knowledge and without desire, and where there are those who have knowledge, to keep them from presuming to act (on it). When there is this abstinance from action, good order is universal.

All things spring up, and there is not one which declines to show itself; they grow, and there is no claim made for their ownership; they go through their processes, and there is no expectation (of a reward for the results). The work is accomplished, and there is no resting in it (as an achievement).

The work is done, but how no one can see;
'Tis this that makes the power not cease to be.

CHAPTER 4
The Fountain Less

The Tao is (like) the emptiness[1] of a vessel; and in our employment of it we must be on our guard against all fulness. How deep and unfathomable it is, as if it were the Honoured Ancestor of all things!

We should blunt our sharp points, and unravel the complications of things; we should attemper our brightness, and bring ourselves into agreement with the obscurity of others. How pure and still the Tao is, as if it would ever so continue!

I do not know whose son it is. It might appear to have been before God.

CHAPTER 5
The Use of Emptiness

Heaven and earth do not act from (the impulse of) any wish to be benevolent; they deal with all things as the dogs of grass are dealt with.[2] The sages do not act from (any wish

---

[1]"Emptiness" in terms of religious knowledge is always a difficult concept to deal with. As used in Chapter 3 ("the sage . . . empties their minds"), the Chinese word stands for an "empty heart," and means "humility" or "open-mindedness." Lin Yutang interprets the phrase as the sign of a cultured gentleman. Yutang writes that throughout the Tao book the word "empty" and "full" are used to mean "humility" and "pride" respectively. But in Chapter 4 and the last paragraph of Chapter 5 *emptiness* is used in a different context than Lin Yutang allows. As James Legge describes it: "The use of emptiness; quiet and unceasing is the operation of the Tao, and effective is the rule of the sage in accordance with it." This description of emptiness is more in the tradition of religious meaning found in many mystical writings—"emptiness" as an expression of ultimate reality —and closer to a true meaning of what Lao Tzu seems to be expressing. For a clear and thorough discussion of this difficult and abstruse aspect of religious "knowing," see *Emptiness A Study in Religious Meaning*, (A Depth Study of the Philosopher Nagarjuna and His Interpretation of Ultimate Reality), by Frederick J. Streng, Abingdon Press, New York, 1967.

[2]The grass dogs were made of straw tied into the shape of dogs and used in rituals when praying for rain. After the sacrifice was over the dogs were thrown away. The meaning conveyed is that heaven and earth and the sages dealt in such a way with all things—in effect, the Sage's perfect impartiality and the pervasive indifference of nature.

to be) benevolent; they deal with the people as the dogs of grass are dealt with.

May not the space between heaven and earth be compared to a bellows?

'Tis emptied, yet it loses not its power;
'Tis moved again, and sends forth air the more.
Much speech to swift exhaustion lead we see;
Your inner being guard, and keep it free.

CHAPTER 6
The Completion of Material Forms

The valley spirit does not, aye the same;
The female mystery thus do we name.[1]
Its gate, from which at first they issued forth,
Is called the root from which grew heaven and earth.
Long and unbroken does its power remain,
Used gently, and without the touch of pain.

CHAPTER 7
Sheathing the Light

Heaven is long-enduring and earth continues long. The reason why heaven and earth are able to endure and continue thus long is because they do not live of, or for, themselves. This is how they are able to continue and endure.

Therefore the sage puts his own person last, and yet it is found in the foremost place; he treats his person as if it were foreign to him, and yet that person is preserved. It is not because he has no personal and private ends, that therefore such ends are realized?

[1] James Legge analyzes this chapter as laying the foundation for the later development in Taoism that deals with the control of breath. The "spirit of the valley" stands for the active or vital force of the Tao, the *teh*, as seen in the title of this book, *Tao Teh Ching*. The "female mystery" is the same symbol seen in Chapter 1 as "the Mother of all things." Lao Tzu is thought to present life here as a process of evolving (instead of "creation" as in Christianity) from a primal force or vital breath, which ultimately divides into two, and appears in the forms of material and immaterial things.

CHAPTER 8
The Placid and Contented Nature

The highest excellence is like (that of) water. The excellence of water appears in its benefiting all things, and in its occupying, without striving (to the contrary), the low place which all men dislike. Hence (its way) is near to (that of) the Tao.

The excellence of a residence is in (the suitability of) the place; that of the mind is in abysmal stillness; that of associations is in their being with the virtuous; that of government is in its securing good order; that of (the conduct of) affairs is in its ability; and that of (the initiation of) any movement is in its timeliness.

And when (one with the highest excellence) does not wrangle (about his low position), no one finds fault with him.

CHAPTER 9
Dangers in Fullness

It is better to leave a vessel unfilled, than to attempt to carry it when it is full. If you keep feeling a point that has been sharpened, the point cannot long preserve its sharpness.

When gold and jade fill the hall, their possessor cannot keep them safe. When wealth and honors lead to arrogancy, this brings its evil on itself. When the work is done, and one's name is becoming distinguished, to withdraw into obscurity is the way of heaven.

CHAPTER 10
Possibilities

When the intelligent and animal souls are held together in one embrace, they can be kept from separating. When one gives undivided attention to the (vital) breath, and brings it to the utmost degree of pliancy, he can become as a (tender) babe. When he has cleansed away the most mysterious sights (of his imagination), he can become without a flaw.

In loving the people and ruling the state, cannot he proceed without any (purpose of) action? In the opening and shutting of his gates of heaven, cannot he do so as a female bird? While his intelligence reaches in every direction, cannot he (appear to) be without knowledge?

(The Tao) produces (all things) and nourishes them; it produces them and does not claim them as its own; it does all, and yet does not boast of it; it presides over all, and yet does not control them. This is what is called "The mysterious Quality" (of the Tao).

CHAPTER 11
The Use of What Has no Substantive Existence

The thirty spokes unite in the one nave; but it is on the empty space (for the axle), that the use of the wheel depends. Clay is fashioned into vessels; but it is on their empty hollowness, that their use depends. The door and windows are cut out (from the walls) to form an apartment; but it is on the empty space (within), that its use depends. Therefore, what has a (positive) existence serves for profitable adaptation, and what has not that for (actual) usefulness.

CHAPTER 12
Repression of the Desires

Color's five hues from th' eyes their sight will take;
Music's five notes the ears as deaf can make;
The flavors five deprive the mouth of taste;[1]
The chariot course, and the wild hunting waste
Make mad the mind; and objects rare and strange,
Sought for, men's conduct will to evil change.

[1]The five tastes are salt, bitter, acrid, and sweet. The five musical notes are those of the Chinese scale, equivalent to our G,A,B,D,E. The five colors are black, red, green or blue, white, and yellow.

Therefore the sage seeks to satisfy (the craving of) the belly, and not the (instatiable longing of the) eyes.[1] He puts from him the latter, and prefers to seek the former.

CHAPTER 13
Loathing Shame

Favor and disgrace would seem equally to be feared; honor and great calamity, to be regarded as personal conditions (of the same kind).

What is meant by speaking thus of favor and disgrace? Disgrace is being in a low position (after the enjoyment of favor). The getting that (favor) leads to the apprehension (of losing it), and the losing it leads to the fear of (still greater calamity):—this is what is meant by saying that favor and disgrace would seem equally to be feared.

And what is meant by saying that honor and great calamity are to be (similarly) regarded as personal conditions? What makes me liable to great calamity is my having the body (which I call myself); if I had not the whole body, what great calamity could come to me?

Therefore he who would administer the kingdom, honoring it as he honors his own person, may be employed to govern it and he who would administer it with the love which he bears to his own person may be entrusted with it.

CHAPTER 14
Manifestation of the Mystery

We look at it, and we do not see it, and we name it "the Equable." We listen to it, and we do not hear it, and we name it "the Inaudible." We try to grasp it, and do not

---

[1]Wang Pi, one of the more renowned Taoist commentators, summarizes and clarifies the Taoist idea here brilliantly: "In satisfying the belly one nourishes himself; in gratifying the eyes he makes a slave of himself." "Belly" is believed to represent the inner self in this phrase, the unconscious and instinctive aspect; while the "eye" is said to refer to the external world and the sensuous self.

get hold of it, and we name it "the Subtle." With these three qualities, it cannot be made the subject of description; and hence we blend them together and obtain The One.

Its upper part is not bright, and its lower part is not obscure. Ceaseless in its action, it yet cannot be named, and then it again returns and becomes nothing. This is called the Form of the Formless, and the Semblance of the Invisible; this is called the Fleeting and Indeterminable.

We meet it and do not see its Front; we follow it, and do not see its Back. When we can lay hold of the Tao of old to direct the things of the present day, and are able to know it as it was of old in the beginning, this is called (unwinding) the clue of Tao.

CHAPTER 15
Exhibition of the Quality

The skillful masters (of the Tao) in old times, with a subtle and exquisite penetration, comprehended its mysteries, and were deep (also) so as to elude men's knowledge. As they were thus beyond men's knowledge, I will make an effort to describe of what sort they appeared to be.

Shrinking looked they like those who wade through a stream in winter; irresolute like those who are afraid of all around them; grave like a guest (in awe of his host); evanescent like ice that is melting away; unpretentious like wood that has not been fashioned into anything; vacant like a valley, and dull like muddy water.

Who can (make) the muddy water (clear)? Let it be still, and it will gradually become clear. Who can secure the condition of rest? Let movement go on, and the condition of rest will gradually arise.

They who preserve this method of the Tao do not wish to be full (of themselves). It is through their not being full of themselves that they can afford to seem worn and not appear new and complete.

CHAPTER 16
Returning to the Root

The (state of) vacancy should be brought to the utmost degree, and that of stillness guarded with unwearying vigor. All things alike go through their processes of activity, and (then) we see them return (to their original state). When things (in the vegetable world) have displayed their luxuriant growth, we see each of them return to its root. This returning to their root is what we call the state of stillness; and that stillness may be called a reporting that they have fulfilled their appointed end.

The report of that fulfillment is the regular, unchanging rule. To know that unchanging rule is to be intelligent; not to know it leads to wild movements and evil issues. The knowledge of that unchanging rule produces a (grand) capacity and forbearance, and that capacity and forbearance lead to a community (of feeling with all things). From this community of feeling comes a kingliness of character; and he who is king-like goes on to be heaven-like. In that likeness to heaven he possesses the Tao. Possessed of the Tao, he endures long; and to the end of his bodily life, is exempt from all danger of decay.

CHAPTER 17
Unadulterated Influence

In the highest antiquity, (the people) did not know that there were (their rulers). In the next age they loved them and praised them. In the next they feared them; in the next they despised them. Thus it was that when faith (in the Tao was deficient (in the rulers) a want of faith in them ensued (in the people).

How irresolute did those (earliest rulers) appear, showing (by their reticence) the importance which they set upon their words! Their work was done and their undertakings were successful, while the people all said, "We are as we are, of ourselves!"

CHAPTER 18
The Decay of Manners

When the Great Tao (Way or Method) ceased to be observed, benevolence and righteousness came into vogue. (Then) appeared wisdom and shrewdness, and there ensued great hypocrisy.

When harmony no longer prevailed throughout the six kinships, filial sons found their manifestation; when the states and clans fell into disorder, loyal ministers appeared.

CHAPTER 19
Returning to the Unadulterated Influence

If we could renounce our sageness and discard our wisdom, it would be better for the people a hundredfold. If we could renounce our benevolence and discard our righteousness, the people would again become filial and kindly. If we could renounce our artful contrivances and discard our (scheming for) gain, there would be no thieves nor robbers.

Those three methods (of government)
Thought olden ways in elegance did fail
And made these names their want of worth to veil;
But simple views, and courses plain and true
Would selfish ends and many lusts eschew.

CHAPTER 20
Being Different from Ordinary Men

When we renounce learning we have no troubles.
The (ready) "yes," and (flattering) "yea";
Small is the difference they display.
But mark their issues, good and ill;
What space the gulf between shall fill?
What all men fear is indeed to be feared; but how wide and without end is the range of questions (asking to be discussed)!

The multitude of men look satisfied and pleased; as if

enjoying a full banquet, as if mounted on a tower in spring. I alone seem listless and still, my desires having as yet given no indication of their presence. I am like an infant which has not yet smiled. I look dejected and forlorn, as if I had no home to go to. The multitude of men all have enough and to spare. I alone seem to have lost everything. My mind is that of a stupid man; I am in a state of chaos.

Ordinary men look bright and intelligent, while I alone seem to be benighted. They look full of discrimination, while I alone am dull and confused. I seem to be carried about as on the sea, drifting as if I had nowhere to rest. All men have their spheres of action, while I alone seem dull and incapable, like a rude borderer. (Thus) I alone am different from other men, but I value the nursing-mother (the Tao).

CHAPTER 21
The Empty Heart

The grandest forms of active force
From Tao come, their only source.
Who can of Tao the nature tell?
Our sight it flies, our touch as well.
Eluding touch, eluding sight,
There are their semblances, all right.
Profound it is, dark and obscure;
Things' essences all there endure.
Those essences the truth enfold
Of what, when seen, shall then be told.
Now it is so; 'twas so of old.
Its name—what passes not away;
So, in their beautiful array,
Things form and never know decay.

How know I that it is so with all the beauties of existing things? By this (nature of the Tao).

CHAPTER 22

The Increase Granted Humility

The partial becomes complete; the crooked, straight; the empty, full; the worn out, new. He whose (desires) are few gets them; he whose (desires) are many goes astray.

Therefore the sage holds in his embrace the one thing (of humility), and manifests it to all the world. He is free from self-display, and therefore he shines; from self-assertion, and therefore he is distinguished; from self-boasting, and therefore his merit is acknowledged; from self-complacency, and therefore he acquires superiority. It is because he is thus free from striving that therefore no one in the world is able to strive with him.

That saying of the ancients that "the partial becomes complete" was not vainly spoken:—all real completion is comprehended under it.[1]

CHAPTER 23

Absolute Vacancy

Abstaining from speech marks him who is obeying the spontaneity of his nature. A violent wind does not last for a whole morning; a sudden rain does not last for the whole day. To whom is it that these (two) things are owing? To heaven and earth. If heaven and earth cannot make such (spasmodic) actings last long, how much less can nam!

Therefore when one is making the Tao his business, those who are also pursuing it, agree with him in it, and

---

[1]Those familiar with the Western mystical religious movement of Quietism will no doubt have already seen many instances of clear similarities between the Taoist and quietist doctrines. But Chapter 22 represents this parallel most clearly. The "emptiness" which becomes full is the cavity in the ground that fills with water. The "worn out" is regenerated anew in the spring, as a bare tree with withered leaves is renewed. It is in stillness that Tao makes itself known; it is in utter quiet, neither praying nor speaking, wishing nor willing, that the Western quietist believes God is most likely to speak (at *His* pleasure). So the Tao speaks to stillness, although Lao Tzu did not imply any personality to Tao as did the quietists.

those who are making the manifestation of its course their object agree with him in that; while even those who are failing in both these things agree with him where they fail.

Hence, those with whom he agrees as to the Tao have the happiness of attaining to it; those with whom he agrees as to its manifestation have the happiness of attaining to it; and those with whom he agrees in their failure have also the happiness of attaining (to the Tao). (But) when there is not faith sufficient (on his part), a want of faith (in him) ensues (on the part of the others).

CHAPTER 24
Painful Graciousness

He who stands on his tiptoes does not stand firm; he who stretches his legs does not walk (easily). (So), he who displays himself does not shine; he who asserts his own views is not distinguished; he who vaunts himself does not find his merit acknowledged; he who is self-conceited has no superiority allowed to him. Such conditions, viewed from the standpoint of the Tao, are like remnants of food, or a tumor on the body, which all dislike. Hence those who pursue (the course) of the Tao do not adopt and allow them.

CHAPTER 25
Representations of the Mystery

There was something undefined and complete, coming into existence before heaven and earth. How still it was and formless, standing alone, and undergoing no change, reaching everywhere and in no danger (of being exhausted)! It may be regarded as the Mother of all things.

I do not know its name, and I give it the designation of the Tao (the Way or Course). Making an effort (further) to give it a name I call it The Great.[1]

---

[1] It is in this chapter that Lao Tzu first "names the nameless," the *Tao*. "He does not know its name," and calls it the "Way," or "Course", and thereby indicates its phenomenal aspects, its evolutionary development. To distinguish it from all other forms of evolution he calls it "the Great Method" and employs the same Chinese character throughout the book

Great, it passes on (in constant flow). Passing on, it becomes remote. Having become remote, it returns. Therefore the Tao is great; heaven is great; earth is great; and the (sage) king is also great. In the universe there are four that are great, and the (sage) king is one of them.

Man takes his law from the earth; the earth takes its law from heaven; heaven takes its law from the Tao. The law of the Tao is its being what it is.

CHAPTER 26
The Quality of Gravity

Gravity is the root of lightness; stillness, the ruler of movement.[1]

Therefore a wise prince, marching the whole day, does not go far from his baggage waggons. Although he may have brilliant prospects to look at, he quietly remains (in his proper place), indifferent to them. How should the lord of a myriad chariots carry himself lightly before the kingdom? If he do act lightly, he has lost his root (of gravity); if he proceeded to active movement, he will lose his throne.

CHAPTER 27
Dexterity in Using

The skillful traveler leaves no traces of his wheels or footsteps; the skillful speaker says nothing that can be found fault with or blamed; the skillful reckoner uses no tallies; the

---

to stand for the Tao. But it is more than simply evolving phenomena and underlying cause—it is also "the Uncaused Cause," it is the "nameless Tao," the "beginning or originating cause of heaven and earth." All other subordinate phenomena, from the invisible to the visible get their force or power from the Tao. It is a spontaneity evolving from and to itself: "It returns. It flows away, far away, and comes back ... It is everywhere." The basis of Taoist quietism is also found here: who can seek out such a thing, "Who can by searching find God? Who can find out the Almighty to perfection?" One cannot find it out, but must be silent and still in mind and spirit to be receptive to its flux.

[1]The gravity and stillness, both attributes of the Tao, are also shown in this chapter to be necessary for the attainment of perfection. As Legge describes it: "He who cultivates it must not give way to lightness of mind, or hasty action." These last two chapters set the foundation of Taoist quietism.

skillful closer needs no bolts or bars, while to open what he has shut will be impossible; the skillful binder uses no strings or knots, while to unloose what he has bound will be impossible. In the same way the sage is always skillful at saving men, and so he does not cast away any man; he is always skillful at saving things, and so he does not cast away anything. This is called "Hiding the light of his procedure."

Therefore the man of skill is a master (to be looked up to) by him who has not the skill; and he who has not the skill is the helper of (the reputation of) him who has the skill. If the one did not honor his master, and the other did not rejoice in his helper, an (observer), though intelligent, might greatly err about them. This is called "The utmost degree of mystery."

CHAPTER 28
Returning to Simplicity

Who knows his manhood's strength,
Yet still his female feebleness maintains;
As to one channel flow the many drains,
All come to him, yea, all beneath the sky.
Thus he the constant excellence retains;—
The simple child again, free from all stains.

Who knows how white attracts,
Yet always keeps himself within black's shade,
The pattern of humility displayed,
Displayed in view of all beneath the sky;
He in the unchanging excellence arrayed,
Endless return to man's first state has made.

Who knows how glory shines,
Yet loves disgrace, nor e'er for it is pale;
Behold his presence in a spacious vale,
To which men come from all beneath the sky.
The unchanging excellence completes its tale;
The simple infant man in him we hail.

The unwrought material, when divided and distributed, forms vessels. The sage, when employed, becomes the Head of all the Officers (of government); and in his greatest regulations he employs no violent measures.

CHAPTER 29
Taking no Action

If any one should wish to get the kingdom for himself, and to effect this by what he does, I see that he will not succeed. The kingdom is a spirit-like thing, and cannot be got by active doing. He who would so win it destroys it; he who would hold it in his grasp loses it.

The course and nature of things is such that
> What was in front is now behind;
> What warmed anon we freezing find.
> Strength is of weakness oft the spoil;
> The store in ruins mocks our toil.

Hence the sage puts away excessive effort, extravagance, and easy indulgence.[1]

CHAPTER 30
A Caveat Against War

He who would assist a lord of men in harmony with the Tao will not assert his mastery in the kingdom by force of arms. Such a course is sure to meet with its proper return.

Wherever a host is stationed, briars and thorns spring up. In the sequence of great armies there are sure to be bad years.

A skillful (commander) strikes a decisive blow, and stops. He does not dare (by continuing his operations) to assert and complete his mastery. He will strike the blow, but will be on his guard against being vain or boastful or arrogant in consequence of it. He strikes it as a matter of necessity; he strikes

---

[1]Here again is an exact statement of the perennial admonition of the quietist—Western or Eastern—to take "no action." The Tao forbids action as does the Western quietist from Molinos to the present. All action of a personal nature, with an ego-driven purpose, will be sure to fail in the largest as well as the smallest of things.

it, but not from a wish for mastery.

When things have attained their strong maturity they become old. This may be said to be not in accordance with the Tao: and what is not in accordance with it soon comes to an end.

CHAPTER 31
Stilling War

Now arms, however beautiful, are instruments of evil omen, hateful, it may be said, to all creatures. Therefore they who have the Tao do not like to employ them.

The superior man ordinarily considers the left hand the most honorable place, but in time of war the right hand. Those sharp weapons are instruments of evil omen, and not the instruments of the superior man;—he uses them only on the compulsion of necessity. Calm and repose are what he prizes; victory (by force of arms) is to him undesirable. To consider this desirable would be to delight in the alaughter of men; and he who delights in the slaughter of men cannot get his will in the kingdom.

On occasions of festivity to be on the left hand is the prized position; on occasions of mourning, the right hand. The second in command of the army has his place on the left; the general commanding in chief has his on the right; —his place, that is, is assigned to him as in the rites of mourning. He who has killed multitudes of men should weep for them with the bitterest grief; and the victor in battle has his place (rightly) according to those rites.

CHAPTER 32
Sagely Virtue[1]

The Tao, considered as unchanging, has no name.

Though in its primordial simplicity it may be small, the whole world dares not deal with (one embodying) it as a

---

[1]Legge did not like this translation of the title for Chapter 32, but found it "difficult to supply a better." Lin Yutang translates it "Tao is Like the Sea".

minister. If a feudal prince or the king could guard and hold it, all would spontaneously submit themselves to him.

Heaven and earth (under its guidance) unite together and send down the sweet dew, which, without the directions of men, reaches equally everywhere as of its own accord.

As soon as it proceeds to action, it has a name. When it once has that name, (men) can know to rest in it. When they know to rest in it, they can be free from all risk of failure and error.

The relation of the Tao to all the world is like that of the great rivers and seas to the streams from the valleys.

CHAPTER 33
Discriminating Between Attributes

He who knows other men is discerning; he who knows himself is intelligent. He who overcomes others is strong; he who overcomes himself is mighty. He who is satisfied with iis lot is rich; he who goes on acting with energy has a (firm) will.

He who does not fail in the requirements of his position, continues long; he who dies and yet does not perish, has longevity.[1]

CHAPTER 34
The Task of Achievement

All-pervading is the Great Tao! It may be found on the left hand and on the right.

All things depend on it for their production, which it gives to them, not one refusing obedience to it. When its work is accomplished, it does not claim the name of having done it. It clothes all things as with a garment, and makes

---

[1]The matter of survival after death has been a primary concern of all religions. A major Chinese belief is here set forward. From the writings of Lieh Tzu, from Chuang Tzu, and even from the extinction of the Buddhists, there can be found the same meaning as represented here by Lao Tzu: that "the human body is like the covering of the caterpillar or the skin of the snake; we occupy it but for a passing sojourn." (James Legge, *Texts of Taoism*, p. 124.)

no assumption of being their lord;—it may be named in the smallest things. All things return (to their root and disappear), and do not know that it is it which presides over their doing so;—it may be named in the greatest things.

Hence the sage is able (in the same way) to accomplish his great achievements. It is through his not making himself great that he can accomplish them.

CHAPTER 35

The Attribute of Benevolence

To him who holds in his hands the Great Image (of the invisible Tao), the whole world repairs. Men resort to him, and receive no hurt, but (find) rest, peace, and the feeling of ease.

Music and dainties will make the passing guest stop (for a time). But though the Tao as it comes from the mouth, seems insipid and has no flavor, though it seems not worth being looked at or listened to, the use of it is inexhaustible.

CHAPTER 36

Minimizing the Light

When one is about to take an inspiration, he is sure to make a (previous) expiration; when he is going to weaken another, he will first strengthen him; when he is going to overthrow another, he will first have raised him up; when he is going to despoil another, he will first have made gifts to him:—this is called "Hiding the light (of his procedure)."

The soft overcomes the hard; and the weak the strong.

Fishes should not be taken from the deep; instruments for the profit of a state should not be shown to the people.

CHAPTER 37

The Exercise of Government

The Tao in its regular course does nothing (for the sake of doing it), and so there is nothing which it does not do.

If princes and kings were able to maintain it, all things

would of themselves be transformed by them.

If this transformation became to me an object of desire,
I would express the desire by the nameless simplicity.

> Simplicity without a name
> Is free from all external aim.
> With no desire, at rest and still,
> All things go right as of their will.

CHAPTER 38
About the Attributes

(Those who) possessed in highest degree the attributes
(of the Tao) did not (seek) to show them, and therefore they
possessed them (in fullest measure). (Those who) possesses
in a lower degree those attributes (sought how) not to lose
them, and therefore they did not possess them (in fullest
measure).

(Those who) possessed in the highest degree those attributes did nothing (with a purpose), and had no need to do
anything. (Those who) possessed them in a lower degree
were (always) doing, and had need to be so doing.

(Those who) possessed the highest benevolence were (always seeking) to carry it out, and had no need to be doing
so. (Those who) possessed the highest righteousness were
(always seeking) to carry it out, and had need to be so doing.

(Those who) possessed the highest (sense of) propriety
were (always seeking) to show it, and when men did not
respond to it, they bared the arm and marched up to
them.

Thus it was that when the Tao was lost, its attributes
appeared; when its attributes were lost, benevolence appeared; when benevolence was lost, righteousness appeared;
and when righteousness was lost, the proprieties appeared.

Now propriety is the attenuated form of leal-heartedness
and good faith, and is also the commencement of disorder;
swift apprehension is (only) a flower of the Tao, and is the
beginning of stupidity.

Thus it is that the Great man abides by what is solid, and

eschews what is flimsy; dwells with the fruit and not with the flower. It is thus that he puts away the one and makes choice of the other.

CHAPTER 39
The Origin of the Law

The things which from of old have got the One (the Tao) are—

Heaven which by it is bright and pure;
Earth rendered thereby firm and sure;
Spirits with powers by it supplied;
Valleys kept full throughout their void;
All creatures which through it do live;
Princes and kings who from it get
The model which to all they give.

All these are the results of the One (Tao).

If heaven were not thus pure, it soon would rend;
If earth were not thus sure, 'twould break and bend;
Without these powers, the spirits soon would fail;
If not so filled, the drought would parch each vale;
Without that life, creatures would pass away;
Princes and kings, without that moral sway,
However grand and high, would all decay.

Thus it is that dignity finds its (firm) root in its (previous) meanness, and what is lofty finds its stability in the lowness (from which it rises). Hence princes and kings call themselves "Orphans," "Men of small virtue," and as "Carriages without a nave." Is not this an acknowledgement that in their considering themselves mean they see the foundation of their dignity? So it is that in the enumeration of the different parts of a carriage we do not come on what makes it answer the ends of a carriage. They do not wish to show themselves elegant-looking as jade, but (prefer) to be coarse-looking as an (ordinary) stone.

CHAPTER 40

Dispensing with the Use of Means

The movement of the Tao
By contraries proceeds;
And weakness marks the course
Of Tao's mighty deeds.

All things under heaven sprang from It as existing (and named); that existence sprang from It as non-existent (and not named).

CHAPTER 41

Sameness and Difference

Scholars of the highest class, when they hear about the Tao, earnestly carry it into practice. Scholars of the middle class, when they have heard about it, seem now to keep it and now to lose it. Scholars of the lowest class, when they have heard about it, laugh greatly at it. If it were not (thus) laughed at, it would not be fit to be the Tao.

Therefore the sentence-makers have thus expressed themselves:—

The Tao, when brightest seen, seems light to lack;
Who progress in it makes, seems drawing back;
Its even way is like a rugged track.
Its highest virtue from the vale doth rise;
Its greatest beauty seems to offend the eyes;
And he has most whose lot the least supplies.
Its firmest virtue seems but poor and low;
Its solid truth seems change to undergo;
Its largest square doth yet no corner show;
A vessel great, it is the slowest made;
Loud is its sound, but never word it said;
A semblance great, the shadow of a shade.

The Tao is hidden, and has no name; but it is the Tao which is skillful at imparting (to all things what they need) and making them complete.

CHAPTER 42
Transformations of the Tao

The Tao produced One; One produced Two; Two produced Three; Three produced All things. All things leave behind them the Obscurity (out of which they have come), and go forward to embrace the Brightness (into which they have emerged), while they are harmonized by the Breath of Vacancy.

What men dislike is to be orphans, to have little virtue, to be as carriages without naves; and yet these are the designations which kings and princes use for themselves. So it is that some things are increased by being diminished, and others are diminished by being increased.

What other men (thus) teach, I also teach. The violent and strong do not die their natural death. I will make this the basis of my teaching.

CHAPTER 43
Use of Action in Weakness[1]

The softest thing in the world dashes against and overcomes the hardest; that which has no (substantial) existence enters where there is no crevice. I know hereby what advantage belongs to doing nothing (with a purpose).

There are few in the world who attain to the teaching without words, and the advantage arising from non-action.

CHAPTER 44
Cautions

Or fame or life,
Which do you hold more dear?

---

[1]Legge's full title, "The Universal Use (of the Action in Weakness of the Tao)" seemed cumbersome. The title chosen here seems to convey adequately the meaning of the chapter—which refers back to Chapter 40: "Weakness marks the course of Tao's mighty deeds." Lin Yutang translates the title far more freely to read: "The Softest Substance."

Or Life or wealth,
   To which would you adhere?
Keep life and lose those other things;
Keep them and lose your life:—which brings
   Sorrow and pain more near?

Thus we may see,
   Who cleaves to fame
   Rejects what is more great;
Who loves large stores
   Gives up the richer state.

Who is content
Needs fear no shame.
Who knows to stop
Incurs no blame.
From danger free
Long live shall he.

CHAPTER 45
Great or Overflowing Virtue

Who thinks his great achievements poor
Shall find his vigor long endure.
Of greatest fullness, deemed a void,
Exhaustion ne'er shall stem the tide.
Do thou what's straight still crooked deem;
They greatest art still stupid seem,
And eloquence a stammering scream.
  Constant action overcomes cold; being still overcomes
heat. Purity and stillness give the correct law to all under
heaven.

CHAPTER 46
Moderating of Desire

When the Tao prevails in the world, they send back their
swift horses to (draw) the dung-carts. When the Tao is
disregarded in the world, the warhorses breed in the border
lands.

There is no guilt greater than to sanction ambition; no calamity greater than to be discontented with one's lot; no fault greater than the wish to be getting. Therefore the sufficiency of contentment is an enduring and unchanging sufficiency.

CHAPTER 47
Surveying the Far-off

Without going outside his door, one understands (all that takes place) under the sky; without looking out from his window, one sees the Tao of Heaven. The farther that one goes out (from himself), the less he knows.

Therefore the sages got their knowledge without traveling; gave their (right) names to things without seeing them; and accomplished their ends without any purpose of doing so.[1]

CHAPTER 48
Forgetting Knowledge

He who devotes himself to learning (seeks) from day to day to increase (his knowledge); he who devotes himself to the Tao (seeks) from day to day to diminish (his doing).

He diminishes it and again diminishes it, till he arrives at doing nothing (on purpose). Having arrived at this point of non-action, there is nothing which he does not do.[2]

---

[1]Legge describes this chapter as "somewhat mystical" and difficult to divine Lao Tzu's full meaning. The most obvious interpretation being that it is a lesson to men to learn to judge things "according to their internal conviction of similar things in their own experience." Lao Tzu seems to imply that man is a microcosm, and if he can learn to understand the movements of his own mind, he can understand the movements of all other minds and the macrocosm (universe) as well.

[2]"Tao proceeds by contraries" is a common Taoist saying. But another major element in Taoism is the process of diminishing. Chiao Hung writes in one of his commentaries on the *Tao Teh Ching:* The wise man "carries on the process of diminishing till there is nothing coarse about him which is not put away. He puts it away till he has forgotten all that was bad in it. He then puts away all that is fine about him. He does so till he has forgotten all that was good in it. But the bad was wrong, and the good is

He who gets as his own all under heaven does so by giving himself no trouble (with that end). If one take trouble (with that end), he is not equal to getting as his own all under heaven.

CHAPTER 49
The Quality of Indulgence

The sage has no invariable mind of his own; he makes the mind of the people his mind.

To those who are not good (to me), I am also good;—and thus (all) get to be good. To those who are sincere (with me), I am sincere; and to those who are not sincere (with me), I am also sincere;—and thus (all) get to be sincere.[1]

The sage has in the world an appearance of indecision, and keeps his mind in a state of indifference to all. The people all keep their eyes and ears directed to him, and he deals with them all as his children.

CHAPTER 50
The Value Set on Life

Men come forth and live; they enter (again) and die.

Of every ten, three are ministers of life (to themselves); and three are ministers of death.

There are also three in every ten whose aim is to live, but whose movements tend to the land (or place) of death. And for what reason? Because of their excessive endeavors to perpetuate life.

But I have heard that he who is skillful in managing the life entrusted to him for a time travels on the land without

---

right. Having diminished the wrong, and also diminished the right, the process is carried on till they are both forgotten. Passion and desire are both cut off; and his virtue and the Tao are in such union that he does nothing; but though he does nothing, he allows all things to do their own doing, and all things are done."

[1]Lao Tzu was the first philosopher, as can be seen in this chapter, to state the ethically sophisticated premise of returning good for evil. Confucius later followed Lao Tzu's example, although not fully. In the Confucian *Analects*, XIV, 36, we find: "Injury should be recompensed with Kindness," a clearly stated Christian doctrine as well.

having to shun rhinoceros or tiger, and enters a host without having to avoid buff coat or sharp weapon. The rhinoceros finds no place in him into which to thrust its horn, nor the tiger a place in which to fix its claws, nor the weapon a place to admit its point. And for what reason? Because there is in him no place of death.

CHAPTER 51

The Operation of Tao in Nourishing Things

All things are produced by the Tao, and nourished by its ourflowing operation. They receive their forms according to the nature of each, and are completed according to the circumstances of their condition. Therefore all things without exception honor the Tao, and exalt its outflowing operation.

This honoring of the Tao and exalting of its operation is not the result of any ordination, but always a spontaneous tribute.

Thus it is that the Tao produces (all things), nourishes them, brings them to their full growth, nurses them, completes them, matures them, maintains them, and overspreads them.

It produces them and makes no claim to the possession of them; it carries them through their processes and does not vaunt its ability in doing so; it brings them to maturity and exercises no control over them;—this is called its mysterious operation.

CHAPTER 52

Returning to the Source

(The Tao) which originated all under the sky is to be considered as the mother of them all.

When the mother is found, we know what her children should be. When one knows that he is his mother's child, and proceeds to guard (the qualities of) the mother that belong to him, to the end of his life he will be free from all peril.

Let him keep his mouth closed, and shut up the portals (of his nostrils), and all his life he will be exempt from laborious exertion. Let him keep his mouth open, and (spend his breath) in the promotion of his affairs, and all his life there will be no safety for him.

The perception of what is small is (the secret of) clear-sightedness; the guarding of what is soft and tender is (the secret of) strength.

Who uses well his light,
Reverting to its (source so) bright,
Will from his body ward all blight,
And hides the unchanging from men's sight.

CHAPTER 53
Increase of Evidence

If I were suddenly to become known, and (put into a position to) conduct (a government) according to the Great Tao, what I should be most afraid of would be a boastful display.

The great Tao (or way) is very level and easy; but people love the by-ways.

Their court(-yards and buildings) shall be well kept, but their fields shall be ill-cultivated, and their granaries very empty. They shall wear elegant and ornamented robes, carry a sharp sword at their girdle, pamper themselves n eating and drinking, and have a superabundance of property and wealth;—such (princes) may be called robbers and boasters. This is contrary to the Tao surely!

CHAPTER 54
The Cultivation of Tao

What (Tao's) skillful plater plants
   Can never be uptorn;
What his skillful arms enfold,
   From him can ne'er be borne.
Sons shall bring in lengthening line,
Sacrifices to his shrine.

Tao when nursed within one's self,
  His vigor will make true;
And where the family it rules
  What riches will accrue!
The neighborhood where it prevails
  In thriving will abound;
And when 'tis seen throughout the state,
  Good fortune will be found.
Employ it the kingdom o'er,
  And men thrive all around.

In this way the effect will be seen in the person, by the observation of different cases; in the family; in the neighborhood; in the state; and in the kingdom.

How do I know that this effect is sure to hold thus all under the sky? By this (method of observation).

CHAPTER 55
The Mysterious Charm

He who has in himself abundantly the attributes (of the Tao) is like an infant. Poisonous insects will not sting him; fierce beasts will not seize him; birds of prey will not strike him.

(The infant's) bones are weak and its sinews soft, but yet its grasp is firm. It knows not yet the union of male and female, and yet its virile member may be excited;—showing the perfection of its physical essence. All day long it will cry without its throat becoming hoarse;—showing the harmony (in its constitution).

To him by whom this harmony is known,
(The secret of) the unchanging (Tao) is shown,
And in the knowledge wisdom finds its throne.
All life-increasing arts to evil turn;
Where the mind makes the vital breath to burn.
(False) is the strength, (and o'er it we should mourn.)

When things have become strong, they (then) become old, which may be said to be contrary to the Tao. Whatever is contrary to the Tao soon ends.

CHAPTER 56

The Mysterious Excellence

He who knows (the Tao) does not (care to) speak (about it); he who is (every ready to) speak about it does not know it.

He (who knows it) will keep his mouth shut and close the portals (of his nostrils). He will blunt his sharp points and unravel the complications of things; he will attemper his brightness, and bring himself into agreement with the obscurity (of others). This is called "the Mysterious Agreement."

(Such an one) cannot be treated familiarly or distnatly; he is beyond all consideration of profit or injury; of nobility or meanness:—he is the noblest man under heaven.[1]

CHAPTER 57

The Genuine Influence

A state may be ruled by (measures of) correction; weapons of war may be used with crafty dexterity; (but) the kingdom is made one's own (only) by freedom from action and purpose.

How do I know that it is so? By these facts:—In the kingdom the multiplication of prohibitive enactments increases the poverty of the people; the more implements to add to their profit that the people have, the greater disorder is there in the state and clan; the more acts of crafty dexterity that men possess, the more do strange contrivances appear; the more display there is of legislation, the more thieves and robbers there are.

---

[1]The man of Tao is shown here as humble, retiring, oblivious of himself and other men. "The noblest man under heaven" as Legge interprets Lao Tzu here: but Lin Yutang writes of the "mysterious excellence," the man of Tao, as part of "the Mystic Unity," submerged in the One. This interpretation also agrees with Legge, however, in that one so absorbed, so oblivious of himself and others may very well be "submerged in the One."

Therefore a sage has said, "I will do nothing (of purpose), and the people will be transformed of themselves; I will be fond of keeping still, and the people will of themselves become correct. I will take no trouble about it, and the people will of themselves become rich; I will manifest no ambition, and the people will of themselves attain to the primitive simplicity."

CHAPTER 58
Transformation According to Circumstances

The government that seems the most unwise,
Oft goodness to the people best supplies;
That which is meddling, touching everything,
Will work but ill, and disappointment bring.
Misery!—happiness is to be found by its side! Happiness!—misery lurks beneath it! Who knows what either will come to in the end?

Shall we then dispense with correction? The (method of) correction shall by a turn become distortion, and the good in it shall by a turn become evil. The delusion of the people (on this point) has indeed subsisted for a long time.

Therefore the sage is (like) a square which cuts no one (with its angles); (like) a corner which injures no one (with its sharpness). He is straightforward, but allows himself no license; he is bright, but does not dazzle.

CHAPTER 59
Guarding the Tao

For regulating the human (in our constitution) and rendering the (proper) service to the heavenly, there is nothing like moderation.

It is only by this moderatin that there is effected an early return (to man's normal state). That early return is what I call the repeated accumulation of the attributes (of the Tao). With that repeated accumulation of those attributes, there comes the subjugation (of every obstacle to such return). Of this subjugation we know not what shall be the limit; and when one knows not what the limit shall be, he may be the ruler of a state.

He who possesses the mother of the state may continue long. His case is like that (of the plant) of which we say that its roots are deep and its flower stalks firm:—this is the way to secure that its enduring life shall long be seen.

CHAPTER 60
Occupying the Throne

Governing a great state is like cooking small fish.

Let the kingdom be governed according to the Tao, and the manes of the departed will not manifest their spiritual energy. It is not that those manes have not that spiritual energy, but it will not be employed to hurt men. It is not that it could not hurt men, but neither does the ruling sage hurt them.

When these two do not injuriously affect each other, their good influences converge in the virtue (of the Tao).

CHAPTER 61
The Attribute of Humility

What makes a great state is its being (like) a low-lying, down-flowing (stream);—it becomes the center to which tend (all the small states) under heaven.

(To illustrate from) the case of all females:—the female always overcomes the male by her stillness. Stillness may be considered (a sort of) abasement.

Thus it is that a great state, by condescending to small states, gains them for itself; and that small states, by abasing themselves to a great state, win it over to them. In the one case the abasement leads to gaining adherents, in the other case to procuring favor.

The great state only wishes to unite men together and nourish them; a small state only wishes to be received by, and to serve, the other. Each gets what it desires, but the great state must learn to abase itself.

CHAPTER 62
Practicing the Tao

Tao has of all things the most honored place.
No treasures give good men so rich a grace;
Bad men it guards, and doth their ill efface.

(Its) admirable words can purchase honor; (its) admirable deeds can raise their performer above others. Even men who are not good are not abandoned by it.

Therefore when the sovereign occupies his place as the Son of Heaven, and he has appointed his three ducal ministers, though (a prince) were to send in a round symbol-of-rank large enough to fill both the hands, and that as the precursor of the team of horses (in the court-yard), such an offering would not be equal to (a lesson of) this Tao, which one might present on his knees.

Why was it that the ancients prized this Tao so much? Was it not because it could be got by seeking for it, and the guilty could escape (from the stain of their guilt) by it? This is the reason why all under heaven consider it the most valuable thing.

CHAPTER 63
Thinking in the Beginning

(It is the way of the Tao) to act without (thinking of) acting; to conduct affairs without (feeling the) trouble of them; to taste without discerning any flavor; to consider what is small as great, and a few as many; and to recompense injury with kindness.

(The master of it) anticipates things that are difficult while they are easy, and does things that would become great while they are small. All difficult things in the world are sure to arise from a previous state in which they were easy, and all great things from one in which they were small. Therefore the sage, while he never does what is great, is able on that account to accomplish the greatest things.

He who lightly promises is sure to keep but little faith;

he who is continually thinking things easy is sure to find them difficult. Therefore the sage sees difficulty even in what seems easy, and so never has any difficulties.

CHAPTER 64
Guarding the Minute

That which is at rest is easily kept hold of; before a thing has given indications of its presence, it is easy to take measures against it; that which is brittle is easily broken; that which is very small is easily dispersed. Action should be taken before a thing has made its appearance; order should be secured before disorder has begun.

The tree which fills the arms grew from the tiniest sprout; the tower of nine stories rose from a (small) heap of earth; the journey of a thousand lî commenced with a single step.

He who acts (with an ulterior purpose) does harm; he who takes hold of a thing (in the same way) loses his hold. The sage does not act (so), and therefore does no harm; he does not lay hold (so), and therefore does not lose his hold. (But) people in their conduct of affairs are constantly ruining them when they are on the eve of success. If they were careful at the end, as (they should be) at the beginning, they would not so ruin them.

Therefore the sage desires what (other men) do not desire, and does not prize things difficult to get; he learns what (other men) do not learn, and turns back to what the multitude of men have passed by. Thus he helps the natural development of all things, and does not dare to act (with an ulterior purpose of his own).

CHAPTER 65
Unmixed Excellence

The ancients who showed their skill in practising the Tao did so, not to enlighten the people, but rather to make them simple and ignorant.

The difficulty in governing the people arises from their having much knowledge. He who (tries to) govern a state by his wisdom is a scourge to it; while he who does not (try to) do so is a blessing.

He who knows these two things finds in them also his model and rule. Ability to know this model and rule constitutes what we call the mysterious excellence (of a governor). Deep and far-reaching is such mysterious excellence, showing indeed its possessor as opposite to others, but leading them to a great conformity to him.

CHAPTER 66
Putting One's Self Last

That whereby the rivers and seas are able to receive the homage and tribute of all the valley streams, is their skill in being lower than they;—it is thus that they are the kings of them all. So it is that the sage (ruler), wishing to be above men, puts himself by his words below them, and, wishing to be before them, places his person behind them.

In this way though he has his place above them, men do not feel his weight, nor though he has his place before them, do they feel it an injury to them.

Therefore all in the world delight to exalt him and do not weary of him. Because he does not strive, no one finds it possible to strive with him.

CHAPTER 67
Three Precious Things

All the world says that, while my Tao is great, it yet appears to be inferior (to other systems of teaching). Now it is just its greatness that makes it seem to be inferior. If it were like any other (system), for long would its smallness have been known!

But I have three precious things which I prize and hold fast. The first is gentleness; the second is economy; and the third is shrinking from taking precedence of others.

With that gentleness I can be bold; with that economy I can be liberal; shrinking from taking precedence of others, I can become a vessel of the highest honor. Now-a-days they give up gentleness and are all for being bold; economy, and are all for being liberal; the hindmost place, and seek only to be foremost;—(of all which the end is) death.

Gentleness is sure to be victorious even in battle, and firmly to maintain its ground. Heaven will save its possessor, by his (very) gentleness protecting him.

CHAPTER 68
Matching Heaven

He who in (Tao's) wars has skill
  Assumes no martial port;
He who fights with most good will
  To rage makes no resort.
He who vanquishes yet still
  Keeps from his foes apart;
He whose hests men most fulfil
  Yet humbly plies his art.

Thus we say, "He ne'er contends,
  And therein is his might."
Thus we say, "Men's wills he bends,
  That they with him unite."
Thus we say, "Like heaven's his ends,
  No sage of old more bright."

CHAPTER 69
Use of the Mysterious Tao

A master of the art of war has said, "I do not dare to be the host (to commence the war); I prefer to be the guest (to act on the defensive). I do not dare to advance an inch; I prefer to retire a foot." This is called marshaling the ranks where there are no ranks; baring the arms (to fight) where there are no arms to bare; grasping the weapon where there is no weapon to grasp; advancing against the enemy where there is no enemy.

There is no calamity greater than lightly engaging in war. To do that is near losing (the gentleness) which is so precious. Thus it is that when opposing weapons are (actually) crossed, he who deplores (the situation) conquers.

CHAPTER 70
The Difficulty of Being Known

My words are very easy to know, and very easy to practice; but there is no one in the world who is able to know and able to practice them.

There is an originating and all-comprehending (principle) in my words, and an authoritative law for the things (which I enforce). It is because they do not know these, that men do not know me.

They who know me are few, and I am on that account (the more) to be prized. It is thus that the sage wears (a poor garb of) hair cloth, while he carries his (signet of) jade in his bosom.

CHAPTER 71
The Disease of Knowing

To know and yet (think) we do not know is the highest (attainment); not to know (and yet think) we do know is a disease.

It is simply by being pained at (the thought of) having this disease that we are preserved from it. The sage has not the disease. He knows the pain that would be inseparable from it, and therefore he does not have it.

CHAPTER 72
Loving One's Self

When the people do not fear what they ought to fear, that which is their great dread will come on them.[1]

Let them not thoughtlessly indulge themselves in their ordinary life; let them not act as if weary of what that life depends on.

---

[1]The "great dread" is death, and that which ought to be feared are the passions and appetites. If one indulgences oneself the life energies are shortened, and this brings about an earlier death.

It is by avoiding such indulgence that such weariness does not arise.

Therefore the sage knows (these things) of himself, but does not parade (his knowledge); loves, but does not (appear to set a) value on, himself. And thus he puts the latter alternative away and makes choice of the former.

CHAPTER 73
Allowing Men to Take Their Course

He whose boldness appears in his daring (to do wrong, in defiance of the laws) is put to death; he whose boldness appears in his not daring (to do so) lives on. Of these two cases the one appears to be advantageous, and the other to be injurious. But

> When heaven's anger smites a man,
> Who the cause shall truly scan?

On this account the sage feels a difficulty (as to what to do in the former case).

It is the way of heaven not to strive, and yet it skillfully overcomes; not to speak, and yet it is skillful in (obtaining) a reply; does not call, and yet men come to it of themselves. Its demonstrations are quiet, and yet its plans are skillful and effective. The meshes of the net of heaven are large; far apart, but letting nothing escape.

CHAPTER 74
Restraining Delusion

The people do not fear death; to what purpose is it to (try to) frighten them with death? If the people were always in awe of death, and I could always seize those who do wrong, and put them to death, who would dare to do wrong?

There is always One who presides over the infliction of death. He who would inflict death in the room of him who so presides over it may be described as hewing wood instead of a great carpenter.[1] Seldom is it that he who undertakes the hewing, instead of the great carpenter, does not cut his own hands!

CHAPTER 75
How Greediness Injures

The people suffer from famine because of the multitude of taxes consumed by their superiors. It is through this that they suffer famine.

The people are difficult to govern because of the (excessive) agency of their superiors (in governing them). It is through this that they are difficult to govern.

The people make light of dying because of the greatness of their labors in seeking for the means of living. It is this which makes them think light of dying. Thus it is that to leave the subject of living altogether out of view is better than to set a high value on it.

CHAPTER 76
A Warning Against Trusting in Strength

Man at his birth is supple and weak; at his death, firm and strong. (So it is with) all things. Trees and plants, in their early growth, are soft and brittle; at their death, dry and withered.

Thus it is that firmness and strength are the concomitants of death; softness and weakness, the concomitants of life.

Hence he who (relies on) the strength of his forces does not conquer; and a tree which is strong will fill the outstretched arms, (and thereby invites the feller.)

Therefore the place of what is firm and strong is below, and that of what is soft and weak is above.

---

[1]Lao Tzu here warns against capital punishment. Legge quotes a Taoist commentator, Ho-shang Kung, who writes with finality, that "It is Heaven, which, dwelling on high and ruling all beneath, takes note of the transgressions of men." "It is Heaven that punishes" is the same admonition in Christianity: "Vengeance is mine" saith the Lord.

CHAPTER 77
The Way of Heaven

May not the Way (or Tao) of Heaven be compared to the (method of) bending a bow?[1] The (part of the bow) which was high is brought low, and what was low is raised up. (So Heaven) diminishes where there is superabundance, and supplements where there is deficiency.

It is the Way of Heaven to dimish superabundance, and to supplement deficiency. It is not so with the way of man. He takes away from those who have not enough to add to his own superabundance.

Who can take his own superabundance and therewith serve all under heaven? Only he who is in possession of the Tao!

Therefore the (ruling) sage acts without claiming the results as his; he achieves his merit and does not rest (arrogantly) in it:—he does not wish to display his superiority.

CHAPTER 78
Things to be Believed

There is nothing in the world more soft and weak than waer, and yet for attacking things that are firm and strong there is nothing that can take precedence of it;—for there is nothing (so effectual) fow hich it can be changed.

Every one in the world knows that the soft overcomes the hard, and the weak the strong, but no one is able to carry it out in practice.

Therefore a sage has said,

[1]There is confusion on the part of translators and commentators alike here on the meaning and significance of the "bending of the bow." Richard Wilhelm thinks, along with Legge, that a strenuous, athletic feat of bending a large bow, analogous perhaps to Ulysses's massive bow that no man could bend but Ulysses, and even then he needed the help of the Gods. Arthur Waley rejects this translation and interpretation and thinks the "act of shooting an arrow" from the bow is meant. Lin Yutang avoids comment entirely.

"He who accepts his state's reproach,
Is hailed therefore its altars' lord;
To him who bears men's direful woes
They all the name of King accord."
Words that are strictly true seem to be paradoxical.

CHAPTER 79

Adherence to Covenant

When a reconciliation is effected (between two parties) after a great animosity, there is sure to be a grudge remaining (in the mind of the one who was wrong). And how can this be beneficial (to the other)?

Therefore (to guard against this), the sage keeps the left-hand portion of the record of the engagement, and does not insist on the (speedy) fulfilment of it by the other party.[1] (So), he who has the attributes (of the Tao) regards (only) the conditions of the engagement, while he who has not those attributes regards only the conditions favorable to himself.

In the Way of Heaven, there is no partiality of love; it is always on the side of the good man.

CHAPTER 80

Standing Alone

In a little state with a small population, I would so order it, that, though there were individuals with the abilities of ten or a hundred men, there should be no employment of them; I would make the people, while looking on death as a grievous thing, yet not remove elsewhere (to avoid it).

Though they had boats and carriages, they should have no occasion to ride in them; though they had buff coats and

---

[1]The Chinese had an intriguing way of settling disputes. As Legge describes it: "The terms of a contract or agreement were inscribed on a slip of wood, which was then divided into two; each party having one half of it. At the settlement, if the halves perfectly fitted to each other, it was carried through." What is meant here though is that the sage sees the whole terms of any dispute, while lesser men see only that aspect which is favorable to themselves. Ultimately, Lao Tzu says, any such question is decided by the action (teh) of Heaven, by the course of Tao.

sharp weapons, they should have no occasion to don or use them.

I would make the people return to the use of knotted cords (instead of the written characters).

They should think their (coarse) food sweet; their (plain) clothes beautiful; their (poor) dwellings places of rest; and their common (simple) ways sources of enjoyment.

There should be a neighboring state within sight, and the voices of the fowls and dogs should be heard all the way from it to us, but I would make the people to old age, even to death, not have any intercourse with in.

CHAPTER 81
The Manifestation of Simplicity[1]

Sincere words are not fine; fine words are not sincere. Those who are skilled (in the Tao) do not dispute (about it); the disputatious are not skilled in it. Those who know (the Tao) are not extensively learned; the extensively learned do not know it.

The sage does not accumulate (for himself). The more that he expends for others, the more does he possess of his own; the more that he gives to others, the more does he have himself.

With all the sharpness of the Way of Heaven, it injures not; with all the doing in the way of the sage he does not strive.

The *Tao Teh Ching* is such an important book, and Lao Tzu's philosophy so influential in Taoism, that to more fully understand it I have included a short but excellent table of

---

[1]This final chapter sums up the essential characteristics of the Tao, simplicity and proceeding of the Tao by contraries. He summarizes in these three short paragraphs the whole of Tao, showing that in all its five thousand characters, "there is nothing beyond what is here said." (See James Legge, *Texts of Taosim*, p. 171, for a fuller commentary on the texts, and the quote of Wu Chang above.)

its main concepts compiled by an exceptional oriental scholar, Wing-tsit Chan. (For a complete exposition of Taoism and Chinese philosophy in general see his *A Source Book in Chinese Philosophy*, Princeton University Press, Princeton, N.J., 1963.) The numbers in the following chart refer to the 81 chapters or sections of the *Tao Teh Ching*.

Being and Non-being: 1, 2, 11, 40
Desires: 3, 19, 34, 37, 57
Female, Water: 8, 10, 20, 25, 28, 52, 55, 59, 78
Government: 3, 17, 26, 29–31, 57, 60, 61, 65, 74, 75, 80
Humanity and Righteousness: 18, 19, 38
Knowledge: 3, 70, 71
Name: 1, 25, 32, 41
Natural *(tzu–jan):* 17, 23, 25, 51, 64
Non-strife: 3, 7–9, 22, 66, 73, 81
One: 10, 14, 22, 39, 42
Relativity, Good and Evil, Paradoxes: 2, 7, 20, 36, 45, 58
Reversal: 14, 16, 28, 40, 52
Simplicity: 19, 28, 32, 37, 57
Tao: 1, 4, 8, 14, 16, 21, 23, 32, 34, 37, 40–42, 51
Tranquillity: 16, 37, 61
Vitue: 10, 21, 23, 38, 51, 65
Weakness: 10, 22, 36, 40, 43, 52, 76, 78
Wu-wei (taking no action): 2, 3, 10, 37, 43, 48, 63, 64

Chuang Tzu
Selections from
the Book of Chuang Tzu

In the northern ocean there is a fish, called the leviathan, many thousand li^1 in size. This leviathan changes into a bird, called the rukh, whose back is many thousand *li* in breadth. With a might effort it rises, and its wings obscure the sky like clouds. At the equinox, this bird prepares to start for the southern ocean, the Celestial Lake. And in the *Record of Marvels* we read that when the rukh flies southwards, the water is smitten for a space of three thousand *li* around, while the bird itself mounts upon a typhoon to a height of ninety thousand *li*, for a flight of six months' duration. Just so are the motes in a sunbeam blown aloft by God. For whether the blue of the sky is its real color, or only the result of distance without end, the effect to the bird looking down would be just the same as to the motes. . . . A cicada laughed, and said to a young dove, "Now, when I fly with all my might, 'tis as much as I can do to get from tree to tree. And sometimes I do not reach, but fall to the ground midway. What, then, can be the use of going up ninety thousand *li* in order to start for the south?" . . . Those two little creatures,—what should they know? Small knowledge has not the compass of great knowledge any more than a short year has the length of a long year. How can we tell that this is so? The mushroom of a morning knows not the alternation of day and night. The chrysalis knows not the alter-

<hr>

[1]The *li* is about one-third of a mile, or 550 yards.

nation of spring and autumn. Theirs are short years. But in the State of Ch'u there is a tortoise whose spring and autumn are each of five hundred years' duration. And in former days there was a large tree which had a spring and autumn each of eight thousand years' duration. Yet P'eng Tsu[1] is still, alas! an object of envy to all.

Tzu Ch'i of Nan-kuo sat leaning on a table. Looking up to heaven, he sighed and became absent, as though sould and body had parted. Yen Ch'eng Tzu Yu, who was standing by him, exclaimed: "What are you thinking about that your body should become thus like dry wood, your mind like dead ashes? Surely the man now leaning on the table s not he who was here just now."

"My friend," replied Tzu Ch'i, "your question is apposite. To-day I have buried myself. . . . Do you understand? . . . Ah! perhaps you only know the music of man, and not that of earth. Or even if you have heard the music of earth, you have not heard the music of heaven."

"Pray explain," said Tzu Yu.

"The breath of the universe," continued Tzu Ch'i, "is called wind. At times, it is inactive. But when active, every aperture resounds to the blast. Have you never listened to its growing roar? Caves and dells of hill and forest, hollows in huge trees of many a span in girth,—these are like nostrils, like mouths, like ears, like beamsockets, like goblets, like mortars, like ditches, like bogs. And the wind goes rushing through them, sniffing, snoring, singing, soughing, puffing, purling, whistling, whirring, now shrilly treble, now deeply bass, now soft, now loud; until, with a lull, silence reigns supreme. Have you never witnessed among the trees such a disturbance as this?"

"Well, then," inquired Tzu Yu, "since the music of earth consists of nothing more than holes, and the music of man

[1]The Chinese Methuselah.

of pipes and flutes, of what consists the music of heaven?"

"The effect of the wind upon these various apertures," replied Tzu Ch'i, "is not uniform. But what is it that gives to each the individuality, to all the potentiality, of sound? . . . Joy and anger, sorrow and happiness, caution and remorse, come upon us by turns, with ever-changing mood. They come like music from hollowness, like mushrooms from damp. Daily and nightly they alternate within us, but we cannot tell whence they spring. Can we then hope in a moment to lay our finger upon their very cause?

"But for these emotions, *I* should not be. But for *me*, they would have no scope. So far we can go; but we do not know what it is that brings theminto play. 'Twould seem to be a *soul;* but the clue to its existence is wanting. That such a power operates is credible enough, though we cannot see its form. It has functions without form.

"Take the human body with all its manifold divisions. Which part of it does a man love best? Does he not cherish all equally, or has he a preference? Do not all equally serve him? And do these servitors then govern themselves, or are they subidivded into rulers and subjects? Surely there is some soulw hich sways them all.

"But whether or not we ascertain what are the functions of this soul, it matters but little to the soul itself. For, coming into existence with this mortal coil its mandate will also be exhausted. To be harassed by the wear and tear of life, and to pass rapidly through it without possibility of arresting one's course,—is not this pitiful indeed? To labor without ceasing, and then, without living to enjy the fruit, worn out, to depart, suddenly, one knows not whither,—is not that a just cause for giref?

"What advantage is there in what men call not dying? The boyd decomposes, and the mind goes with it. This is our real cause for sorrow. Can the world be so dull as not to see this? Or is it I alone who am dull, and others not so? . . . There is nothing which is not objective: there is nothing which is not subjective. But it is impossible to start from the objective. Only from subjective knowledge is it possible to proceed to objective knowledge. Hence it has been said, 'The objective emanates from the subjective; the subjective is consequent upon the objective. This is the Alternation Theory.' Nevertheless, when one is born, the other dies. When one is possible, the other is impossible. When one is affirmative, the other is negative. Which being the case, the true sage rejects all distinctions of this and that. He takes his refuge in God, and places himself in subjective relation with all things.

"And inasmuch as the subjective is also objective, and the objective also subjective, and as the countraries under each are indistinguishably blended, does it not become impossible for us to say whether subjective and objective really exist at all?

"When subjective and objective are both without their correlates, that is the very axis of Tao. And when that axis passes through the center at which all Infinites converge, positive and negative alike blend into an infinite One. . . . Therefore it is that, viewed from the standpoint of Tao, a beam and a pillar are identical. So are ugliness and beauty, greatness, wickedness, perverseness, and strangeness. Separation is the same as construction: construction is the same as destruction. Nothing is subject either to construction or to destruction, for these conditions are brought together into One.

"Only the truly intelligent understand this principle of the identity of all things. They do not view things as apprehended by themselves, subjectively; but transfer themselves into the position of the things viewed. And viewing them thus they are able to comprehend them, nay, to master them; and he who can master them is near.[1] So it is that to place oneself in subjective relation with externals, without consciousness of their objectivity,—this is Tao. But to wear out one's intellect in an obstinate adherence to the individu-

[1]To the great goal of Tao.

ality of things, not recognizing the fact that all things are One,—this is called *Three in the Morning.*"

"What is *Three in the Morning?*" asked Tzu Yu.

"A keeper of monkeys," replied Tzu Chi, "said with regard to their rations of chestnuts, that each monkey was to have three in the morning and four at night. But at this the monkeys were very angry, so the keeper said they might have four in the morning and three at night, with which arrangement they were all well pleased. The actual number of the chestnuts remained the same, but there was an adaptation to the likes and dislikes of those concerned. Such is the principle of putting oneself into subjective relation with externals.

"Wherefore the true sage, while regarding contraries as identical, adapts himself to the laws of heaven. This is called following two courses at once.

"The knowledge of the men of old had a limit. It extended back to a period when matter did not exist. That was the extreme point to which their knowledge reached. The second period was that of matter, but of matter unconditioned. The third epoch saw matter conditioned, but contraries were still unknown. When these appeared, Tap began to decline. And with the decline of Tao, individual bias arose."

It was the time of autumn floods. Every stream poured into the river, which swelled in its turbid course. The banks receded so far from each other that it was impossible to tell a cow from a horse.

Then the Spirit of the River laughed for joy that all the beauty of the earth was gathered to himself. Down with the stream he journeyed east until he reached the ocean. There, looking eastwards and seeing no limit to its waves, his countenance changed. And as he gazed over the expanse, he sighed and said to the Spirit of the Ocean, "A vulgar proverb says that he who has heard but part of the truth thinks no one equal to himself. And such a one am I.

"When formerly I heard people detracting from the learning of Confucius or underrating the heroism of Poh I, I did not believe. But now that I have looked upon your inexhaustibility—alas for me had I not reached your abode, I should have been for ever a laughing-stock to those of comprehensive enlightenment!"

To which the Spirit of the Ocean replied: "You cannot speak of ocean to a well-frog,—the creature of a narrower sphere. You cannot speak of ice to a summer insect,—the creature of a season. You cannot speak of Tao to a pedagogue: his scope is too restricted. But now that you have emerged from your narrow sphere and have seen the great ocean, you know your own insignificance, and I can speak to you of great principles. . . .

"The Four Seas—are they not to the universe but like puddles in a marsh? The Middle Kingdom—is it not to the surrounding ocean like a tare-seed in a granary? Of all the myriad created things, man is but one. And of all those who inhabit the land, live on the fruit of the earth, and move about in cart and boat, an individual man is but one. Is not he, as compared with all creation, but as the tip of a hair upon a horse's skin?

"Dimensions are limitless; time is endless. Conditions are not invariable; terms are not final. Thus, the wise man looks into space, and does not regard the small as too little, nor the great as too much; for he knows that there is no limit to dimension. He looks back into the past, and does not grieve over what is far off, nor rejoice over what is near; for he knows that time is without end. He investigates fullness and decay, and does not rejoice if he succeeds, nor lament if he fails; for he knows that conditions are not invariable. He who clearly apprehends the scheme of existence does not rejoice over life, nor repine at death; for he knows that terms are not final.

"What man knows is not to be compared with what he does not know. The span of his existence is not to be compared with the span of his non-existence. With the small, to strive to exhaust the great necessarily lands him in confusion, and he does not attain his object. How then should one be able to say that the tip of a hair is the *ne plus ultra* of smallness, or that the universe is the *ne plus ultra* of greatness?"

꽃

How do I know that love of life is not a delusion after all? How do I know but that he who dreads to die is as a child who has lost the way and cannot find his home?

The lady Li Chi was the daughter of Ai Feng. When the Duke of Chin first got her, she wept until the bosom of her dress was drenched with tears. But when she came to the royal residence, and lived with the Duke, and ate rich food, she repented of having wept. How then do I know but that the dead repent of having previously clung to life?

Those who dream of the banquet wake to lamentation and sorrow. Those who dream of lamentation and sorrow wake to join the hunt. While they dream, they do not know that they dream. Some will even interpret the very dream they are dreaming; and only when they awake do they know it was a dream. By and by comes the Great Awakening, and then we find out that this life is really a great dream. Fools think they are awake now, and flatter themselves they know if they are really princes or peasants. Confucius and you are both dreams; and I who say you are dreams,—I am but a dream myself. This is a paradox. Tomorrow a sage may arise to explain it; but that tomorrow will not be until ten thousand generations have gone by.

Granting that you and I argue. If you beat me, and not I you, are you necessarily right and I wrong? Or if I beat you and not you me, am I necessarily right and you wrong? Or are we both partly right and partly wrong? Or are we both wholly right or wholly wrong? You and I cannot know this, and consequently the world will be in ignorance of the truth.

Who shall I employ as arbiter between us? If I employ some one who takes your view, he will side with you. How can such a one arbitrate between us? If I employ some one who takes my view, he will side with me. How can such a one arbitrate between us? And if I employ some one who either differs from or agrees with both of us, he will be equally unable to decide between us. Since then you, and I, and man, cannot decide, must we not depend upon Another? Such dependence is as though it were not dependence. We are embraced in the obliterating unity of God.

Once upon a time, I, Chuang Tzu, dreamt I was a butterfly, fluttering hither and thither, to all intents and purposes a butterfly. I was conscious only of following my fancies as a butterfly, and was unconscious of my individuality as a man. Suddenly I awakened, and there I lay, myself again. Now I do not know whether I was then a man dreaming I was a butterfly, or whether I am not a butterfly dreaming I am a man. Between a man and a butterfly there is necessarily a barrier. The transition is called metempsychosis.

The Penumbra said to the Umbra, "At one moment you move: at another you are at rest. At one moment you sit down: at another you get up. Why this instability of purpose?"

"I depend," replied the Umbra, "upon something which causes me to do as I do; and that something depends in turn upon something else which causes it to do as it does. My dependence is like that of a snake's scales or of a cicada's wings. How can I tell why I do one thing, or why I do not do another?"

A disciple said to Lu Chü: "Master, I have attained to your Tao. I can do without fire in winter. I can make ice in summer."

"You merely avail yourself of latent heat and latent cold," replied Lu Chü. "That is not what I call Tao. I will demonstrate to you what my Tao is."

Thereupon he tuned two lutes, and placed one in the hall and the other in the adjoining room. And when he struck the *kung* note on one, the *kung* note on the other sounded; when he struck the *chio* note on one, the *chio* note on the other sounded. This because they were both tuned to the same pitch.

But if he changed the interval of one string, so that it no longer kept its place in the octave, and then struck it, the result was that all the twenty-five strings jangled together. There was sounds as before, but the influence of the keynote was gone.

Prince Hui's cook was cutting up a bullock. Every blow of his hand, every heave of his shoulders, every tread of his foot, every thrust of his knee, every *whshh* of rent flesh, every *chhk* of the chopper, was in perfect harmony,—rhythmical like the dance of the Mulberry Grove, simultaneous like the chords of the Ching Shou.

"Well done!" cried the Prince; "yours is skill indeed."

"Sire," replied the cook, "I have always devoted myself to Tao. It is better than skill. When I first began to cut up bullocks, I saw before me simply *whole* bullocks. After three years' practice, I saw no more whole animals. And now I work with my mind and not with my eye. When my senses bid me stop, but my mind urges me on, I fall back upon eternal principles. I follow such openings or cavities as there may be, according to the natural constitution of the animal.

I do not attempt to cut through joints: still less through large bones.[1]

"A good cook changes his chopper once a year,—because he cuts. An ordinary cook, once a month,—because he hacks. But I have had this chopper nineteen years, and although I have cut up many thousand bullocks, its edge is as if fresh from the whetstone. For at the joints there are always interstices, and the edge of a chopper being without thickness, it remains only to insert that which is without thickness into such an interstice. By these means the interstice will be enlarged, and the blade will find plenty of room. It is thus that I have kept my chopper for nineteen years as though fresh from the whetstone.

"Nevertheless, when I come upon a hard part where the blade meets with a difficulty, I am all caution. I fix my eye on it. I stay my hand, and gently apply my blade, until with a *hwah* the part yields like earth crumbling to the ground. Then I take out my chopper, and stand up, and look around, and pause, until with an air of triumph I wipe my chopper and put it carefully away."

"Bravo!" cried the Prince. "From the words of this cook I have learnt how to take care of my life."

In the State of Cheng there was a wonderful magician named Chi Han. He knew all about birth and death, gain and loss, misfortune and happiness, long life and short life —predicting events to a day with supernatural accuracy. The people of Cheng used to flee at his approach; but Lieh Tzu went to see him, and became so infatuated that on his return he said to Hu Tzu,[2] "I used to look upon your Tao as perfect. Now I know something more perfect still."

[1] A reference to Lao Tzu: "That which has no substance enters where there is no crevice."
[2] His tutor.

"So far," replied Hu Tzu, "I have only taught you the ornamentals, not the essentials, of Tao; and yet you think you know all about it. Without cocks in your poultry-yard, what sort of eggs do the hens lay?[1] If you go about trying to force Tao down people's throats, you will be simply exposing yourself. Bring your friend with you, and let me show myself to him."

So next day Lieh Tzu went with Chi Han to see Hu Tzu, and when they came out Chi Han said: "Alas! your teacher is doomed. He canot live. I hardly give him ten days. I am astonished at him. He is but wet ashes."

Lieh Tzu went in and wept bitterly, and told Hu Tzu; but the latter said: "I showed myself to him just now as the earth shows us its outward form, motionless and still, while production is all the time going on. I merely prevented him from seeing my pent-up energy within. Bring him again."

Next day the interview took place as before; but as they were leaving Chi Han said to Lieh Tzu: "It is lucky for your teacher that he met me. He is better. He will recover. I saw he had recuperative power."

Lieh Tzu went in and told Hu Tzu; whereupon the latter replied: "I showed myself to him just now as heaven shows itself in all its dispassionate grandeur, letting a little energy run out of my heels. He was thus able to detect that I had some. Bring him here again."

Next day a third interview took place, and as they were leaving, Chi Han said to Lieh Tzu: "Your teacher is never one day like another; I can tell nothing from his physiognomy. Get him to be regular, and I will then examine him again."

This being repeated to Hu Tzu as before, the latter said: "I showed myself to him just now in a state of harmonious equilibrium. Where the whale disports itself,— is the abyss. Where water is in motion,—is the abyss.

[1]Giles writes: "The hens here stand for the letter of the doctrine; the cocks, for its spirit; and the eggs, for a real knowledge of it."

The abyss has nine names. These are three of them."[1]

Next day the two went once more to see Hu Tzu; but Chi Han was unable to stand still, and in his confusion turned and fled.

"Pursue him!" cried Hu Tzu; whereupon Lieh Tzu ran after him, but could not overtake him; so he returned and told Hu Tzu that the fugitive had disappeared.

"I showed myself to him just now," said Hu Tzu, "as Tao appeared before time was. I was to him as a great blank, existing of itself. He knew not who I was. His face fell. He became confused. And so he fled."

Upon this Lieh Tzu stood convinced that he had not yet acquired any real knowledge, and at once set to work in earnest, passing three years without leaving the house. He helped his wife without leaving the house. He helped his wife to cook the family dinner, and fed his pigs just like human beings. He discarded the artificial and reverted to the natural. He became merely a shape. Amidst confusion he was unconfounded. And so he continued to the end.

Books are what the world values as representing Tao. But books are only words, and the valuable part of words is the thought therein contained. That thought has a certain bias which cannot be conveyed in words, yet the world values words as being the essence of books. But though the world values them, they are not of value; as that sense in which the world values them is not the sense in which they are valuable. . . .

Duke Huan was one day reading in his hall, when a wheelwright who was working below flung down his hammer and chisel, and mounting the steps said: "What words may your Highness be studying?"

"I am studying the words of the sages," replied the Duke.

[1]That is, the three phases of Tao. It will be seen throughout the Taoist portion of the writings that Lao Tzu's favorite symbols for the characteristics of the Tao are the qualities of water.

"Are the sages alive?" asked the wheelwright.

"No," answered the Duke; "they are dead."

"Then the words your Highness is studying," rejoined the wheelwright, "are only the dregs of the ancients."

"What do you mean, sirrah!" cried the Duke, "by interfering with what I read? Explain yourself, or you shall die."

"Let me take an illustration," said the wheelwright, "from my own trade. In making a wheel, if you work too slowly, you can't make it firm; if you work too fast, the spokes won't fit in. You must go neither too slowly nor too fast. There must be co-ordination of mind and hand. Words cannot explain what it is, but there is some mysterious art herein. I cannot teach it to my son; nor can he learn it from me. Consequently, though seventy years of age, I am still making wheels in my old age. If the ancients, together with what they could not impart, are dead and gone, then what your Highness is studying must be the dregs."

Tao has its laws and its evidences. It is devoid both of action and of form. It may be transmitted, but cannot be received. It may be obtained, but cannot be seen. Before heaven and earth were, Tao was. It has existed without change from all time. Spiritual beings drew their spirituality therefrom, while the universe became what we can see it now. To Tao, the zenith is not high, nor the nadir low; no point in time is long ago, nor by lapse of ages has it grown old.

Hsi Wei[1] obtained Tao, and so set the universe in order. Fu Hsi[2] obtained it, and was able to establish eternal princi-

[1]A mythical personage.

[2]Fu Hsi is the first Chinese monarch of major importance. An almost legendary figure, he was supposed to have flourished around 2852 B.C., and has been traditionally credited with the creation of the original lines (*yin* and *yang*) of the *I Ching*, and their symbolic significance. For a more complete description of this, see a new edition of the *I Ching*, edited and arranged by Raymond Van Over, (New York: New American Library, Mentor Books, 1971).

ples. The Great Bear obtained it, and has never erred from
its course. The sun and moon obtained it, and have never
ceased to revolve.

Chuang Tzu said: "O my exemplar! Thou who destroyest
all things, and dost not account it cruelty; thou who benefit-
est all time, and doest not account it charity; thou who art
older than antiquity and dost not account it age; thou who
supportest the universe, shaping the many forms therein,
and dost not account it skill; this is the happiness of
God!"

The universe is very beautiful, yet it says nothing. The
four seasons abide by a fixed law, yet they are not heard. All
creation is based upon absolute principles, yet nothing
speaks.

And the true sage, taking his stand upon the beauty of
the universe, pierces the principles of created things. Hence
the saying that the perfect man does nothing, the true sage
performs nothing, beyond gazing at the universe.

For man's intellect, however keen, face to face with the
countless evolutions of things, their death and birth, their
squareness and roundness,—can never reach the root. There
creation is, and there it has ever been.

The six cardinal points, reaching into infinity, are ever
included in Tao. An autumn spikelet, in all its minuteness,
must carry Tao within itself. There is nothing on earth
which does not rise and fall, but it never perishes altogether.
The *Yin* and the *Yang*,[1] and the four seasons, keep to their
proper order. Apparently destroyed, yet really existing; the
material gone, the immaterial left,—such is the law of creation which passeth all understanding. This is called the root,
whence a glimpse may be obtained of God.

[1]The positive and negative principles of Chinese cosmogony.

A man's knowledge is limited; but it is upon what he does not know that he depends to extend his knowledge to the apprehension of God.

Knowledge of the great One, of the great Negative, of the great Nomenclature, of the great Uniformity, of the great Space, of the great Truth, of the great Law,—this is perfection. The great One is omnipresent. The great Negative is omnipotent. The great Nomenclature is all-inclusive. The great Uniformity is all-assimilative. The great Space is all-receptive. The great Truth is all-exacting. The great Law is all-binding.

The ultimate end is God. He is manifested in the laws of nature. He is the hidden spring. At the beginning, he was. This, however, is inexplicable. It is unknowable. But from the unknowable we reach the known.

Investigation must not be limited, nor must it be unlimited. In this undefinedness there is an actuality. Time does not change it. It cannot suffer diminution. May we not, then, call it our great Guide?

Why not bring our doubting hearts to investigation thereof? And then, using certainty to dispel doubt, revert to a state without doubt, in which doubt is doubly dead?

"Chi Chen," said Shao Chih, "taught *Chance;* Chieh Tzu taught *Predestination.* In the speculations of these two schools, on which side did right lie?"

"The cock crows," replied Tai Kung Tiao, "and the dog barks. So much we know. But the wisest of us could not say why one crows and the other barks, nor guess why they crow or bark at all.

"Let me explain. The infinitely small is inappreciable; the infinitely great is immeasurable. Chance and predestination must refer to the conditioned. Consequently, both are wrong.

"Predestination involves a real existence. Chance implies an absolute absence of any principle. To have a name and the embodiment thereof,—this is to have a material existence. Chance implies an absolute absence of any principle. To have a name and the embodiment thereof,—this is to have a material existence. To have a neme and the embodiment thereof,—this is to have a material existence. To have no name and no embodiment,—of this one can speak and think; but the more one speaks the farther off one gets.

"The unborn creature cannot be kept from life. The dead cannot be tracked. From birth to death is but a span; yet the secret cannot be known. Chance and predestination are but *a priori* solutions.

"When I seek for a beginning, I find only time infinite. When I look forward to an end, I see only time infinite. Infinity of time past and to come implies no beginning and is in accordance with the laws of material existences. Predestination and chance give us a beginning, but one which is compatible only with the existence of matter.

"Tao cannot be existent. If it were existent, it could not be non-existent. The very name of Tao is only adopted for convenience' sake. Predestination and chance are limited to material existences. How can they bear upon the infinite?

"Were language adequate, it would take but a day fully to set forth Tao. Not being adequate, it takes that time to explain material existences. Tao is something beyond material existences. It cannot be conveyed either by words or by silence. In that state which is neither speech nor silence, its transcendental nature may be apprehended."

All things spring from germs. Under many diverse forms these things are ever being reproduced. Round and round, like a wheel, no part of which is more the starting-point than any other. This is called heavenly equilibrium. And he who holds the scales is God.

When Lao Tzu died, Ch'in Shih went to mourn. He uttered three yells and departed.

A disciple asked him, saying: "Were you not our Master's friend?"

"I was," replied Ch'in Shih.

"And if so, do you consider that a sufficient expression of grief at his loss?" added the disciple.

"I do," said Ch'in Shih. "I had believed him to be the man of all men, but now I know that he was not. When I went in to mourn, I found old persons weeping as if for their children, young ones wailing as if for their mothers. And for him to have gained the attachment of those people in this way, he too must have uttered words which should not have been spoken, and dropped tears which should not have been shed, thus violating eternal principles, increasing the sum of human emotion, and forgetting the source from which his own life was received. The ancients called such emotions the trammels of mortality. The Master came, because it was his time to be born; he went, because it was his time to die. For those who accept the phenomenon of birth and death in this sense, lamentation and sorrow have no place. The ancients spoke of death as of God cutting sown a man suspended in the air. The fuel is consumed, but the fire may be transmitted, and we know not that it comes to an end.

To have attained to the human form must be always a source of joy. And then, to undergo countless transitions, with only the infinite to look forward to,—what incomparable bliss is that! Therefore it is that the truly wise rejoice in that which can never be lost, but endures alway.

A son must go whithersoever his parents bid him. Nature is no other than a man's parents. If she bid me die quickly, and I demur, then I am an unfilial son. She can do me no wrong. Tao gives me this form, this toil in manhood, this repose in old age, this rest in death. And surely that which is such a kind arbiter of my life is the best arbiter of my death.

Suppose that the boiling metal in a smelting-pot where to bubble up and say: "Make of me an Excalibur"; I think the caster would reject that metal as uncanny. And if a sinner like myself were to say to God: "Make of me a man, make of me a man"; I think he too would reject me as uncanny. The universe is the smelting-pot, and God is the caster. I shall go whithersoever I am sent, to wake unconscious of the past, as a man wakes from a dreamless sleep.

Chuang Tzu one day saw an empty skull, bleached, but still preserving its shape. Striking it with his riding-whip, he said: "Wert thou once some ambitious citizen whose inordinate yearnings brought him to this pass?—some statesman who plunged his country into ruin and perished in the fray? —some wretch who left behind him a legacy of shame?— some beggar who died in the pangs of hunger and cold? Or didst thou reach this state by the natural course of old age?"

When he had finished speaking, he took the skull and, placing it under his head as a pillow, went to sleep. In the night he dreamt that the skull appeared to him and said: "You speak well, sir; but all you say has reference to the life of mortals, and to mortal troubles. In death there are none of these. Would you like to hear about death?"

Chuang Tzu having replied in the affirmative, the skull began: "In death there is no sovereign above, and no subject below. The workings of the four seasons are unknown. Our existences are bounded only by eternity. The happiness of a king among men cannot exceed that which we enjoy."

Chuang Tzu, however, was not convinced, and said: "Were I to prevail upon God to allow your body to be born again, and your bones and flesh to be renewed, so that you could return to your parents, to your wife, and to the friends of your youth,—would you be willing?"

At this the skull opened its eyes wide and knitted its brows and said: "How should I cast aside happiness greater than that of a king, and mingle once again in the toils and troubles of mortality?"

How does the sage seat himself by the sun and moon, and hold the universe in his grasp? He blends everything into one harmonious whole, rejecting the confusion of this and that. Rank and precedence, which the vulgar prize, the sage stolidly ignores. The revolutions of ten thousand years leave his unity unscathed. The universe itself may pass away, but he will flourish still.

With the truly wise, wisdom is a curse, sincerity like glue, virtue only a means to acquire, and skill nothing more than a commercial capacity. For the truly wise make no plans, and therefore require no wisdom. They do not separate, and therefore require no glue. They want nothing, and therefore need no virtue. They sell nothing, and therefore are not in want of a commercial capacity. These four qualifications are bestowed upon them by God and serve as heavenly food to them. And those who thus feed upon the divine have little need for the human. They wear the forms of men, without human passions. Because they wear the forms of men, they associate with men. Because they have not human passions, positives and negatives find them no place. Infinitesimal, indeed, is that which makes them man; infinitely great is that which makes them divine!

Hui Tzu said to Chuang Tzu: "Are there, then, men who have no passions?"

Chuang Tzu replied: "Certainly."

"But if a man has no passions," argued Hui Tzu, "what is it that makes him a man?"

"Tao," replied Chuang Tzu, "gives him his expression, and God gives him his form. How should he not be a man?"

"If, then, he is a man," said Hui Tzu, "how can he be without passions?"

"What you mean by passions," answered Chuang Tzu, "is not what I mean. By a man without passions I mean one who does not permit good and evil to disturb his internal economy, but rather falls in with whatever happens, as a matter of course, and does not add to the sum of his mortality."

He who knows what God is, and who knows what man is, has attained. Knowing what God is, he knows that he himself proceeded therefrom. Knowing what man is, he rests in the knowledge of the unknown. Working out one's allotted span, and not perishing in mid career,—this is the fulness of knowledge.

Herein, however, there is a flaw. Knowledge is dependent upon fulfilment. And as this fulfilment is uncertain, how can it be known that my divine is not really human, my human really divine? We must have *pure men*, and then only can we have *pure knowledge*.

But what is a pure man?—The pure men of old acted without calculation, not seeking to secure results. They laid no plans. Therefore, failing, they had no cause for regret; succeeding, no cause for congratulation. And thus they could scale heights without fear; enter water without becoming wet; fire, without feeling hot. So far had their wisdom advanced towards Tao.

The pure men of old slept without dreams, and waked without anxiety. They ate without discrimination, breathing deep breaths. For pure men draw breath from their uttermost depths; the vulgar only from their throats. Out of the crooked, words are retched up like vomit. If men's passions are deep, their divinity is shallow.

The pure men of old did not know what it was to love

life nor to hate death. They did not rejoice in birth, nor
strive to put off dissolution. Quickly come and quickly go;
—no more. They did not forget whence it was they had
sprung, neither did they seek to hasten their return thither.
Cheerfully they played their allotted parts, waiting patiently
for the end. This is what is called not to lead the heart astray
from Tao, nor to let the human seek to supplement the
divine. And this is what is meant by a pure man.

The pure men of old did their duty to their neighbors,
but did not associate with them. They behaved as though
wanting in themselves, but without flattering others. Naturally rectangular, they were not uncompromisingly hard.
They manifested their independence without going to extremes. They appeared to smile as if pleased, when the
expression was only a natural response. Their outward semblance derived its fascination from the store of goodness
within. They seemed to be of the world around them, while
proudly treading beyond its limits. They seemed to desire
silence, while in truth they had dispensed with language.
They saw in penal laws a trunk;[1] in social ceremonies,
wings;[2] in wisdom, a useful accessory; in mortality, a guide.
For them penal laws meant a merciful administration; social
ceremonies, a passport through the world; wisdom, an ex-
cuse for doing what they could not help; and morality,
walking like others upon the path. And thus all men praised
them for the worthy lives they led.

The repose of the sage is not what the world calls repose.
His repose is the result of his mental attitude. All creation
could not disturb his equilibrium: hence his repose. When
water is still, it is like a mirror, reflecting the beard and the

---

[1] A natural basis of government.
[2] To aid man's progress through life.

eyebrows. It gives the accuracy of the water-level, and the philosopher makes it his model. And if water thus derives lucidity from stillness, how much more the faculties of the mind! The mind of the sage, being in repose, becomes the mirror of the universe, the speculum of all creation.

The truly great man, although he does not injure others, does not credit himself with charity and mercy. He seeks not gain, but does not despise his followers who do. He struggles not for wealth, but does not take credit for letting it alone. He asks help from no man, but takes no credit for his self-reliance, neither does he despise those who seek preferment through friends. He acts differently from the vulgar crowd, but takes no credit for his exceptionality; nor, because others act with the majority, does he despise them as hypocrites. The ranks and emoluments of the world are to him no cause for joy; its punishments and shame no cause for disgrace. He knows that positive and negative cannot be distinguished, that great and small cannot be defined.

The true sage ignores God. He ignores man. He ignores a beginning. He ignores matter. He moves in harmony with his generation and suffers not. He takes things as they come and is not overwhelmed. How are we to become like him?

The true sage is a passive agent. If he succeeds, he simply feels that he was provided by no effort of his own with the energy necessary to success.

External punishments are inflicted by metal and wood. Internal punishments are inflicted by anxiety and remorse. Fools who incur external punishment are treated with metal or wood. Those who incur internal punishment are devoured by the conflict of emotions. It is only the pure and perfect man who can succeed in avoiding both.

When Chuang Tzu's wife died, Hui Tzu went to condole. He found the widower sitting on the ground, singing, with his legs spread out at a right angle, and beating time on a bowl.

"To live with your wife," exclaimed Hui Tzu, "and see your eldest son grow up to be a man, and then not to shed a tear over her corpse,—this would be bad enough. But to drum on a bowl, and sing; surely this is going too far."

"Not at all," replied Chuang Tzu. "When she died, I could not help being affected by her death. Soon, however, I remembered that she had already existed in a previous state before birth, without form, or even substance; that while in that unconditioned condition, substance was added to spirit; that this substance then assumed form; and that the next stage was birth. And now, by virtue of a further change, she is dead, passing from one phase to another like the sequence of spring, summer, autumn and winter. And while she is thus lying asleep in eternity, for me to go about weeping and wailing would be to proclaim myself ignorant of these natural laws. Therefore I refrain."

When Chuang Tzu was about to die, his disciples expressed a wish to give him a splendid funeral. But Chuang Tzu said: "With heaven and earth for my coffin and shell; with the sun, moon, and stars, as my burial regalia; and with all creation to escort me to the grave,—are not my funeral paraphernalia ready to hand?"

"We fear," argued the disciples, "lest the carrion kite should eat the body of our Master;" to which Chuang Tzu replied: "Above ground I shall be food for kites; below I shall be food for mole-crickets and ants. Why rob one to feed the other?"

惢

Life follows upon death. Death is the beginning of life. Who knows when the end is reached? The life of man results from convergence of the vital fluid. Its convergence is life; its dispersion, death. If, then, life and death are but consecutive states, what need have I to complain? Therefore all things are One.

The I Amplifications
Selections from
The Great Treatise
of the I Ching

The sages set forth the diagrams, inspected the emblems
contained in them, and appended their explanations;—in
this way the good fortune and bad (indicated by them) were
made clear.

The strong and the weak (lines) displace each other, and
produce the changes and transformations (in the figures).

Therefore the good fortune and evil (mentioned in the
explanations) are the indications of the right and wrong (in
men's conduct of affairs), and the repentance and regret
(similarly mentioned) are the indications of their sorrow and
anxiety.

The changes and transformations (of the lines) are the
emblems of the advance and retrogression (of the vital force
in nature). Thus what we call the strong and the weak (lines)
become the emblems of day and night. The movements
which take place in the six places (of the hexagram) show
the course of the three extremes (i.e. of the three Powers in
their perfect operation).

Therefore what the superior man rests in, in whatever
position he is placed, is the order shown in the *I;* and the
study which gives him the greatest pleasure is that of the
explanations of the several lines.

Therefore the superior man, when living quietly, contemplates the emblems and studies the explanations of them;

when initiating any movement, he contemplates the
changes (that are made in divining), and studies the progos-
tications from them. Thus "is help extended to him from
Heaven; there will be good fortune, and advantage in every
movement."

※

The *I* was made on a principle of accordance with heaven
and earth, and shows us therefore, without rent or confusion, the course (of things) in heaven and earth.

(The sage), in accordance with (the *I*), looking up, contemplates the brilliant phenomena of the heavens, and,
looking down, examines the definite arrangements of the
earth;—thus he knows the causes of darkness (or, what is
obscure) and light (or, what is bright). He traces things to
their beginning, and follows them to their end;—thus he
knows what can be said about death and life. (He perceives
how the union of) essence and breath form things, and the
(disappearance or) wandering away of the soul produces the
change (of their constitution):—thus he knows the characteristics of the *anima* and *animus*.

There is a similarity between him and heaven and earth,
and hence there is no contrariety in him to them. His
knowledge embraces all things, and his course is (intended
to be) helpful to all under the sky;—and hence he falls into
no error. He acts according to the exigency of circumstances
without being carried away by their current; he rejoices in
Heaven and knows its ordinations;—and hence he has no
anxieties. He rests in his own (present) position, and
cherishes (the spirit of) generous benevolence;—and hence
he can love (without reserve).

(Through the *I*), he comprehends as in a mold or enclo-
sure the transformations of heaven and earth without any
error; by an ever-varying adaptation he completes (the nature of) all things without exception; he penetrates to a
knowledge of the course of day and night (and all other
connected phenomena);—it is thus that his operation is

spirit-like, unconditioned by place, while the changes which he produces are not restricted to any form.

The successive movement of the inactive and active operations constitutes what is called the course (of things).

That which ensues as the result (of their movement) is goodness; that which shows it in its completeness is the natures (of men and things).[1]

The benevolent see it and call it benevolence. The wise see it and call it wisdom. The common people, acting daily according to it, yet have no knowledge of it. Thus it is that the course (of things), as seen by the superior man, is seen by few.

It is manifested in the benevolence (of its operations), and (then again) it conceals and stores up its resources. It gives their stimulus to all things, without having the same anxieties that possess the sage. Complete is its abundant virtue and the greatness of its stores!

Its rich possessions is what is intended by 'the greatness of its stores;' the daily renovation which it produces is what is meant by 'the abundance of its virtue.'

Production and reproduction is what is called (the process of) change.

The formation of the semblances (shadowy forms of things) is what we attribute to Ch'ien; the giving to them their specific forms is what we attribute to K'un.

The exhaustive use of the numbers (that turn up in manipulating the stalks), and (thereby) knowing (the character of) coming events, is what we call prognosticating; the comprehension of the changes (indicated leads us to) what we call the business (to be done).

That which is unfathomable in (the movement of) the inactive and active operations is (the presence of a) spiritual (power).

[1]The imperial editors tell us that the germ of Mencius's doctrine on the goodness of human nature is found in this paragraph. But the sinologist, James Legge, writes that it more likely means that "every creature is good," and not just man.

Yes, wide is the *I* and great! If we speak of it in its farthest reaching, no limit can be set to it; if we speak of it with reference to what is near at hand, (its lessons are) still and correct; if we speak of it in connection with all between heaven and earth, it embraces all.

There is Ch'ien. In its (individual) stillness it is self-absorbed; when exerting its motive power it goes straight forward; and thus it is that its productive action is on a grand scale. There is K'un. In its (individual) stillness, it is self-collected and capacious; when exerting its motive power, it developes its resources, and thus its productive action is on a wise scale.

In its breadth and greatness, (the *I*) corresponds to heaven and earth; in its ever-recurring changes, it corresponds to the four seasons; in its mention of the bright or active, and the dark or inactive operation, it corresponds to the sun and moon; and the excellence seen in the ease and ready response (of its various operations) corresponds to the perfect operations(presented to us in the phenomena of nature).

The Master said:—'Is not the *I* a perfect book?' It was by the *I* that the sages exalted their virtue, and enlarged their sphere of occupation. Their wisdom was high, and their rules of conduct were solid. That loftiness was after the pattern of heaven; that solidity, after the pattern of earth.

Heaven and earth having their positions as assigned to them, the changes (of nature) take place between them. The nature (of man) having been completed, and being continually preserved, it is the gate of all good courses and righteousness.

The sage was able to survey all the complex pheonmena under the sky. He then considered in his mind how they could be figured, and (by means of the diagrams) represented their material forms and their character. Hence this (diagrams) are denominated Semblances (or emblematic figures, the Hsiang).

A (later) sage was able to survey the motive influences

working all under the sky. He contemplated them in their common action and special nature, in order to bring out the standard and proper tendency of each. He then appended his explanation (to each line of the diagrams), to determine the good or evil indicated by it. Hence those (lines with their explanations) are denominated Imitations (the Yao).

(The diagrams) speak of the most complex phenomena under the sky, and yet there is nothing in them that need awaken dislike; the explanations of the lines speak of the subtlest movements under the sky, and yet there is nothing in them to produce confusion.

The Master said:—'He who knows the method of change and transformation may be said to know what is done by that spiritual (power).'

In the *I* there are four things characteristic of the way of the sages. We should set the highest value on its explanations to guide us in speaking; on its changes for (the initiation of) our movements; on its emblematic figures for (definite action as in) the construction of implements; and on its prognostications for our practice of divination.

Therefore, when a superior man is about to take action of a more private or of a public character, he asks (the *I*), making his inquiry in words. It receives his order, and the answer comes as the echo's response. Be the subject remote or near, mysterious or deep, he forthwith knows of what kind will be the coming result. (If the *I*) were not the most esquisite thing under heaven, would it be concerned in such an operation as this?

(The stalks) are manipulated by threes and fives to determine (one) change; they are laid on opposite sides, and placed one up, one down, to make sure of their numbers; and the (three necessary) changes are gone through with in this way, till they form the figures pertaining to heaven or to earth. Their numbers are exactly determined, and the emblems of (all things) under the sky are fixed. (If the *I*) were not the thing most capable of change of all things under heaven, how could it effect such a result as this?

In (all these operations forming) the *I*, there is no thought and no action. It is still and without movement; but, when acted on, it penetrates forthwith to all phenomena and events under the sky. If it were not the most spirit-like thing under the sky, how could it be found doing this?

The (operations forming the) *I* are the method by which the sages searched out exhaustively what was deep, and investigated the minutest springs (of things).

'Those operations searched out what was deep:'—therefore they could penetrate to the views of all under the sky. 'They made apparent the minutest springs of (things):'—therefore they could bring to a completion all undertakings under the sky. 'Their action was spirit-like:'—therefore they could make speed without hurry, and reached their destination without traveling.

This is the import of what the Master said, that 'in the *I* there are four things indicating the way of the sages.'

The Master said:—'What is it that the *I* does? The *I* opens up (the knowledge of the issues of) things, accomplishes the undertakings (of men), and embraces under it (the way of) all things under the sky. This and nothing more is what the *I* does. Thereby the sages, through (divination by) it, would give their proper course to the aims of of all under the sky, would give stability to their undertakings, and determine their doubts.'

Therefore the virtue of the stalks is versatile and spirit-like; that of the diagrams is exact and wise; and the meaning viven by the six lines is changeful to give (the proper information to men). The sages having, by their possession of these (three virtues), cleansed their minds, retired and laid them up in the secrecy (of their own consciousness). But their sympathies were with the people in regard both to their good fortune and evil. By their spirit-like ability they knew (the character of) coming events, and their wisdom had stored up (all experiences of) the past. Who could be able to accomplish all this? (Only our) ancient sages, quick in apprehension and clear in discernment, of far-reaching intelligence, and all-embracing knowledge, and with a majesty, going spirit-like to its objects;—it was only they who could do so.

Therefore (those sages), fully understanding the way of Heaven, and having clearly ascertained the experience of the oepple, instituted (the employment of) these spirit-like things, as a provision for the use of the people. The sages went about the employment of them (moreover) by purifying their hearts and with reverent caution, thereby giving (more) spirituality and intelligence to their virtue.

Thus, a door shut may be pronounced (analogous to) K'un (or the inactive condition), and the opening of the door (analogous to) Ch'ien (or the active condition). The opening succeeding the being shut may be pronounced (analogous to what we call) a change; and the passing from one of these states to the other may be called the constant course (of things).

The (first) appearance of anything (as a bud) is what we call a semblance; when it has received its complete form, we call it a definite thing.

(The divining-plant having been produced, the sages) set it apart and laid down the method of its employment,—what we call the laws (of devination). The advantage arising from it in external and internal matters, so that the people all use it, stamps it with a character which we call spirit-like.

Therefore in (the system of) the *I* there is the Grand Terminus, which produced the two elementary Forms. Those two Forms produced the Four emblematic Symbols, which again produced the eight Trigrams.

The eight trigrams served to determine the good and evil (issues of events), and from this determination was produced the (successful prosecution of the) great business (of life).

Therefore of all things that furnish models and visible figures that are none greater than heaven and earth; of things that change and extend in influence (on others) there are none greater than the four seasons; of things suspended (in the sky) with their figures displayed clear and bright, there are none greater than the sun and moon; of the honored and exalted there are none greater than he who is the rich and noble (one); in preparing things for practical use, and inventing and making instruments for the benefit of all under the sky, there are none greater than the sages; to explore what is complex, search out what is hidden, to hook up what lies deep, and reach to what is distant, thereby determining (the issues) for good or ill of all events under the sky, and making all men under heaven full of strenuous endeavours, there are no (agencies) greater than those of the stalks and the tortoise-shell.

Therefore Heaven produced the spirit-like things, and the sages took advantage of them. (The operations of) heaven and earth are marked by (so many) changes and transformations; and the sages imitated them (by means of the *I*). Heaven hangs out its (brilliant) figures from which are seen good fortune and bad, and the sages made their emblematic interpretations accordingly. The Ho gave forth the map, and the Lo the writing, of (both of) which the sages took advantage.

In the (scheme of the) *I* there are the four symbolic figures by which they inform men (in divining of the lines making up the diagrams); the explanations appended to them convey the significance (of the diagrams and lines); and the determination (of the divination) as fortunate or the reverse, to settle the doubts (of men).

It is said in the *I*, 'Full of anxious thoughts you go and come; (only) friends will follow you and think with you.' The Master said:—'In all (the processes taking place) under heaven, what is there of thinking? what is there of anxious scheming? They all come to the same (successful) issue, though by different paths; there is one result, though there might be a hundred anxious schemes. What is there of thinking? what is there of anxious scheming?'

The sun goes and the moon comes; the moon goes and the sun comes;—the sun and moon thus take the place each of the other, and their shining is the result. The cold goes and the heat comes; the heat goes and the cold comes;—it is by this mutual succession of the cold and heat that the year is completed. That which goes becomes less and less, and that which comes waxes more and more;—it is by the influence on each other of this contraction and expansion that the advantages (of the different conditions) are produced.[1]

When the looper coils itself up, it thereby straightens itself again; when worms and snakes go into the state of hybernation, they thereby keep themselves alive. (So), when we minutely investigate the nature and reasons (of things), till we have entered into the inscrutable and spirit-like in them, we attain to the largest practical application of them; when that application becomes the quickest and readiest, and all personal restfulness is secured, our virtue is thereby exalted.

Going on beyond this, we reach a point which it is hardly possible to know. We have thoroughly comprehended the inscrutable and spirit-like, and know the processes of transformation;—this is the fulness of virtue.

The *I* is a book which should not be let slip from the mind. Its method (of teaching) is marked by the frequent changing (of its lines). They change and move without staying (in one place), flowing about into any one of the six

---

[1]The *I* is the symbol of change. It was formed in ancient Chinese script from the character for "the sun" placed over that for "the moon." It was observed that as the sun gave way to the moon, and the moon to the sun, so was the cycle of the universe fulfilled. Such change was always evident, it was believed, in the phenomena of nature, the character of man, and the experiences of society.

places of the hexagram. They ascend and descend, ever inconstant. The strong and the weak lines change places, so that an invariable and compendious rule cannot be derived from them;—it must vary as their changes indicate.

The goings forth and comings in (of the lines) are according to rule and measure. (People) learn from them in external and internal affairs to stand in awe.

(The book), moreover, makes plain the nature of anxieties and calamities, and the causes of them. Though (its students) have neither master nor guardian, it is as if their parents drew near to them.

Beginning with taking note of its explanations, we reason out the principles to which they point. We thus find out that it does supply a constant and standard rule. But if there be not the proper men (to carry this out), the course cannot be pursued without them.

The *I* is a book of wide comprehension and great scope, embracing everything. There are in it the way of heaven, the way of man, and the way of earth. It then takes (the lines representing) those three Powers, and doubles them till they amount to six. What these six lines show is simply this,— the way of the three Powers.

This way is marked by changes and movements, and hence we have the imitative lines. Those lines are of different grades (in the trigrams), and hence we designate them from their component elements. These are mixed together, and elegant forms arise. When such forms are not in their appropriate places, the ideas of good fortune and bad are thus produced.

(The sages, who are thus represented, and who made the *I*,) were able to rejoice in heart (in the absolute truth of things), and were able (also) to weigh carefully all matters that could occasion anxiety; (thus) they fixed the good and bad fortune (of all things) under the sky, and could accomplish the things requiring strenuous efforts.

Therefore amid the changes and transformations (taking place in heaven and earth), and the words and deeds of men, events that are to be fortunate have their happy omens. (The sages) knew the definite principles underlying the prognostications of the former class, and the future of those of the latter, (now to be) ascertained by divination.

The places of heaven and earth (in the diagrams) having been determined, the sages were able (by means of the *I*) to carry out and complete their ability. (In this way even) the common people were able to share with them in (deciding about) the counsels of men and the counsels of spiritual beings.

The eight trigrams communicate their information by their emblematic figures. The explanations appended to the lines and the completed figures tell how the contemplation of them affected (the makers). The strong and the weak lines appear mixed in them, and (thus) the good and the evil (which they indicate) can be seen.

The changes and movements (which take place in the manipulation of the stalks and the formation of the diagrams) speak as from the standpoint of what is advantageous. The (intimations of) good and evil vary according to the place and nature (of the lines). Thus they may indicate a mutual influence (in any two of them) of love or hatred, and good or evil is the result; or that mutual influence may be affected by the nearness of the lines to, or their distance from each other, and then repentance or regret is the result; or the influence may be that of truth or of hypocrisy, and then the result is what is advantageous, or what is injurious.

Part 2
TAOISM

Part 2
TAOISM

The Classic of the Harmony of the Seen and Unseen

If one observes the Way of Heaven, and maintains Its do-ings (as his own),[1] all that he has to do is accomplished.

To heaven there belong the five (mutual) foes,[2] and he who sees them (and understands their operation) ap-prehends how they produce prosperity. The same five foes are in the mind of man, and when he can set them in action after the manner of heaven, all space and time are at his disposal, and all things receive their transformations from his person.

The nature of heaven belongs (also) to man; the mind of man is a spring (of power). When the Way of heaven is established, the (Course of) man is thereby determined.

[1]Some Taoists explain the "Way of Heaven" to coincide with the last line of Chapter 9 of the *Tao Teh Ching:* "When the work is done, and one's name has become distinguished, to withdraw into obscurity is the Way of Heaven." To explain the "doings of Heaven" phrase, the first hexagram of the *I Ching* is pointed to: "Heaven in its motion gives the first idea of strength. In accordance with this, the superior man nerves himself to ceaseless activity." For further notes see James Legge, *Sacred Books of the East*, Oxford University Press, (London), Volume XL, Appendix II.

[2]"Foes" here refers to the "five elements" which are believed by Taoists to make up the whole realm of nature—hence, the "Heaven" of the text includes "earth." According to Taoist teaching the element of earth gener-ates metal, and overcomes water; metal generates water, and overcomes wood; water generates wood, and overcomes fire; wood generates fire, and overcomes earth. The cycle is completed, and yet these elements strive together till by such interaction a harmony of the influences arises—and the production goes on "with vigor and beauty."

When heaven puts forth its power of putting to death, the stars and constellations lie hidden in darkness. When earth puts forth its power of putting to death, dragons and serpents appear on the dry ground. When man puts forth his power of putting to death, heaven and earth resume their (proper course). When heaven and man exert their powers in concert, all transformations have their commencements determined.[1]

The nature (of man) is here clever and there stupid; and the one of these qualities may lie hidden in the other. The abuse of the nine apertures if (chiefly) in the three most important, which may be now in movement and now at rest. When fire arises in wood, the evil, having once begun, is sure to go on to the destruction of the wood. When calamity arises in a state, if thereafter movement ensue, it is sure to go to ruin.[2]

When one conducts the work of culture and refining wisely we call him a sage.

CHAPTER 2

For Heaven now to give life and now to take it away is the method of the Tao. Heaven and earth are the despoilers of all things; all things are the despoilers of man; and man is the despoiler of all things. When the three despoilers act as they ought to do, as the three Powers, they are at rest. Hence it is said, "During the time of nourishment, all the members are properly regulated; when the springs of motion come into play, all transformations quietly take place."

Men know the mysteriousness of the Spirit's (action), but

[1]"The power of putting to death" here indicates the moment of quiet, the point of "rest" just after and just prior to movement.

[2]Taoists hold that the constitution of man is twofold—his mental character, quiet and restful, and his physical constitution, restless and addicted to activity. The "nine apertures" are the eyes, ears, nostrils, mouth, the genitalia and anus—and of these, the eyes, ears and mouth are believed to be the most important. But they all need to be kept under restraint. If indulged, ruin of the body and mind is sure to ensue.

they do not know how what is not Spiritual comes to be so. The sun and moon have their definite times, and their exact measures as large and small. The service of the sages hereupon arises, and the spiritual intelligence becomes apparent.

The spring by which the despoilers are moved is invisible and unknown to all under the sky. When the superior man has got it, he strengthens his body by it; when the small man has got it, he makes light of his life.[1]

CHAPTER 3

The blind hear well, and the deaf see well. To derive all that is advantageous from one source is ten times better than the employment of a host; to do this thrice in a day and night is a myriad times better.[2]

The mind is quickened (to activity) by (external) things, and dies through (excessive pursuit of) them. The spring (of the mind's activity) is in the eyes.

Heaven has no (special feeling of) kindness, but so it is that the greatest kindness comes from It. The crash of thunder and the blustering wind both come without design.

Perfect enjoyment is the overflowing satisfaction of the nature. Perfect stillness is the entire disinterestedness of it. When Heaven seems to be most wrapt up in Itself, Its operation is universal in its character.

It is by its breath that we control whatever creature we grasp. Life is the root of death, and death is the root of life. Kindness springs from injury, and injury springs from kind-

[1] James Legge's interpretation of this paragraph seems accurate: "The thing is good in itself, but its effect will be according to the character of its user, and of the use to which it is put."

[2] This phrase is believed by Legge to be taken from the seventh hexagram in the *I Ching*. It indicates that the loss of one sense may be compensated for by greater cultivation of another. Legge interprets it exclusively in physical terms but it seems clearly to relate to behavior and conduct as well, which can be seen in the next paragraph: "The spring of the mind's activity" is through the physical senses. Hence, the mind's activity can be corrupted by extension.

ness. He who sinks himself in water or enters amidst fire brings destruction on himself.

The stupid man by studying the phenomena and laws of heaven and earth becomes sage; I by studying their times and productions become intelligent. He in his stupidity is perplexed about sageness; I in my freedom from stupidity am the same. He considers his sageness as being an extraordinary attainment; I do not consider mine so.

The method of spontaneity proceeds in stillness, and so it was that heaven, earth, and all things were produced. The method of heaven and earth proceeds gently and gradually, and thus it is that the Yin and Yang overcome (each other by turns). The one takes the place of the other, and so change and transformation proceed accordingly.

Therefore the sages, knowing that the method of spontaneity cannot be resisted, take action accordingly and regulate it (for the purpose of culture). The way of perfect stillness cannot be subjected to numerical calculations; but it would seem that there is a wonderful machinery, by which all the heavenly bodies are produced, the eight diagrams, and the sexagenary cycle; spirit-like springs of power, and hidden ghostlinesses; the arts of the Yin and Yang in the victories of the one over the other:—all these come brightly forward into visibility.[1]

[1]These last four sayings are illustrations of Lao Tzu's "contraries" of Taoism. The last paragraph illustrates that whatever is done with design is contrary to the Tao itself. The Taoist sage Li Hsi-yueh summarizes the Yin Fu (The Classic of Harmony of the Seen and the Unseen) in a short paragraph translated by James Legge (ibid., Volume XL, p. 706): "The subject-matter of the Yin Fu and Tao Teh is all intended to set forth the action by contraries of the despoiling powers in nature and society. As to finding in them directions for the government of states, the conduct of war, and the mastery of the kingdom, with such expressions as those about a wonderful machinery by which the heavenly bodies are produced, the eight diagrams, the cycle, spirit-like springs, and hidden ghostlinesses:—they all have a deep meaning, but men do not know it. They who go to the Yin Fu for direction in war and use Lao Tzu for guidance in government go far astray from the meaning of both."

The Classic of Purity

CHAPTER 1

Lao the Master said, The Great Tao has no bodily form,
but It produced and nourishes heaven and earth. The Great
Tao has no passions[1], but It causes the sun and moon to
revolve as they do.

The Great Tao has no name, but It effects the growth
and maintenance of all things.

I do not know its name, but I make an effort, and call It
the Tao.[2]

Now, the Tao (shows itself in two forms); the Pure and
the Turbid, and has (the two conditions of) motion and rest.
Heaven is pure and earth is turbid; heaven moves and earth
is at rest. The masculine is pure and the feminine is turbid;
the masculine moves and the feminine is still. The radical
(Purity) descended, and the (turbid) issue flowed abroad;
and thus all things were produced.

The pure is the source of the turbid, and motion is the
foundation of rest.

If man could always be pure and still, heaven and earth
would both revert (to non-existence).[3]

Now the spirit of man loves Purity, but his mind disturbs
it. The mind of man loves stillness, but his desires draw it

---

[1]"Passions" here refers to the feelings, affections—as it is referred to
in the first of the thirty-nine articles.

[2]All of these references to characteristics of Taoism can be made clear
by turning to the Tao classic, the *Tao Teh Ching*, included in this anthology.

[3]Legge feels he does not understand this paragraph, but translates it as
clearly as he can. In another translation, it is rendered: "If a man is able
to remain pure and motionless, heaven and earth will both at once come
and dwell in him."

away. If he could always send his desires away, his mind would of itself become still. Let his mind be made clean, and his spirit will of itself become pure.

As a matter of course the six desires will not arise, and the three poisons will be taken away and disappear.[1]

The reason why men are not able to attain to this, is because their minds have not been cleansed, and their desires have not been sent away.

If one is able to send the desires away, when he then looks in at his mind, it is no longer his; when he looks out at his body, it is no longer his; and when he looks farther off at external things, they are things which he has nothing to do with.

When he understands these three things, there will appear to him only vacancy. This contemplation of vacancy will awaken the idea of vacuity. Without such vacuity there is no vacancy.

The idea of vacuous space having vanished, that of nothingness itself also disappears; and when the idea of nothingness has disappeared, there ensues serenely the condition of constant stillness.

In that condition of rest independently of place how can any desire arise? And when no desire any longer arises, there is the True stillness and rest.

That True (stillness) becomes (a) constant quality, and responds to external things (without error); yea, that True and Constant quality holds possession of the nature.

In such constant response and constant stillness there is the constant Purity and Rest.

He who has this absolute Purity enters gradually into the (inspiration of the) True Tao. And having entered thereinto, he is styled Possessor of the Tao.

Although he is styled Possessor of the Tao, in reality he

[1]The "six desires" are those stimulated by the eyes, ears, nostrils, the tongue, the sense of touch, and the imagination. The "three poisons" to be cleansed are greed, anger, and stupidity or ignorance.

does not think that he has become possessed of anything. It is as accomplishing the transformation of all living things, that he is styled Possessor of the Tao.

He who is able to understand this may transmit to others the Sacred Tao.

CHAPTER 2

Lao the Master said, Scholars of the highest class do not strive (for anything); those of the lowest class are fond of striving. Those who possess in the highest degree the attributes (of the Tao) do not show them; those who possess them in a low degree hold them fast and display them are not styled (Possessors of) the Tao and Its attributes.

The reason why all men do not obtain the True Tao is because their minds are perverted. Their minds being perverted, their spirits become perturbed. Their minds being perturbed, they are attracted towards external things. Being attracted towards external things, they begin to seek for them greedily. This greedy quest leads to perplexities and annoyances; and these again result in disordered thoughts, which cause anxiety and trouble to both body and mind. The parties then meet with foul disgraces, flow wildly on through the phases of life and death, are liable constantly to sink in the sea of bitterness, and for ever lose the True Tao.

The true and Abiding Tao! They who understand it naturally obtain it. And they who come to understand the Tao abide in Purity and Stillness.

The Classic of
the Pivot of Jade

1. The Heaven-honoured One[1] says, All you, Heaven-endowed men, who wish to be instructed about the Perfect Tao, the Perfect Tao is very recondite, and by nothing else but Itself can it be described. Since ye wish to hear about it, ye cannot do so by the hearing of the ear:—that which eludes both the ears and eyes is the True Tao; what can be heard and seen perishes, and only this survives. There is (much) that you have not yet learned, and especially you have not acquired this! Till you have learned what the ears do not hear, how can the Tao be spoken about at all?

2. The Heaven-honoured One says, Sincerity is the first step towards (the knowledge of) the Tao; it is by silence that that knowledge is maintained; it is with gentleness that (the Tao) is employed. The employment of sincerity looks like stupidity; the employment of silence looks like difficulty of utterance; the employment of gentleness looks like want of ability. But having attained to this, you may forget all bodily form; you may forget your personality; you may forget that you are forgetting.[2]

3. He who has taken the first steps toward (the knowledge of) the Tao knows where to stop; he who maintains the Tao in himself knows how to be diligently vigilant; he who employs It knows what is most subtle.

---

[1]"Heaven Honoured" is a title given by the Taoists to the objects of reverence and worship. "Heaven-endowed men" here indicates "the men possessed by the Tao."

[2]Another scholar, Li Hsi-yueh, describes this state as "the achievement of vacuity, an illustration of the freedom from purpose which is characteristic of the Tao."

When one knows what is most subtle, the light of intelligence grows (around him); when he can know how to be diligently vigilant, his sage wisdom becomes complete; when he knows where to stop, he is grandly composed and restful.

When he is grandly composed and restful, his sage wisdom becomes complete; when his sage wisdom becomes complete, the light of intelligence grows (around him); when the light of intelligence grows around him, he is one with the Tao.

This is the condition which is styled the True Forgetfulness;—a forgetting which does not forget; a forgetting of what cannot be forgotten.

That which cannot be forgotten is the True Tao. The Tao is in heaven and earth, but heaven and earth are not conscious of It. Whether It seem to have feelings or to be without them, It is (always) one and the same.

4. The Heaven-honoured One says, While I am in this world, what shall I do to benefit life? I occupy myself with this subtle and precious Treatise for the good of you, Heaven-endowed men. Those who understand it will be allowed to ascend to the happy seats of the Immortals.

Students of the Tao believe that there are (the influences of) the ether and of destiny. But the (conditions of) climate being different, the constitutions received by men are naturally different, and hence they are ascribed to the ether. And the (conditions of) wisdom and stupidity being different, their constitutions as fine and coarse are naturally different, and hence they are ascribed to the destiny. The destiny depends on fate; the ether depends on heaven.

The restraints arising from the ether and destiny are the manacles decreed by heaven. But if one acquire the True Tao, though stupid, he may become wise; though coarse, he may become fine;—if there only be the decree of fate.

Stupidity the darkest, and coarseness the densest, are consequences of climate; but the suffering of them and the changing of them may take place, when heaven and earth quicken the motive spring. When this is done without the knowledge of men, it is said to take place spontaneously. If it be done with a consciousness of that want of knowledge, it is still said to take place spontaneously. The mystery of spontaneity is greater than that of knowledge; but how it comes to be what it is remains a thing unknown. But as to the Tao, It has not begun to come under the influence of what makes stupid and coarse. Hear this all ye Heaven (-endowed) men; and let all the multitude in all quarters rejoice.

Writings from Lieh Tzu

Dream and Reality

A man of the State of Cheng was one day gathering fuel,
when he came across a startled deer, which he pursued and
killed. Fearing lest any one should see him, he hastily concealed the carcass in a ditch and covered it with plaintain-
leaves, rejoicing excessively at his good fortune. By-and-by,
he forgot the place where he had put it; and, thinking he
must have been dreaming, he set off towards home, hum-
ming over the affair on his way.

Meanwhile, a man who had overheard his words, acted
upon them, and went and got the deer. The latter, when he
reached his house, told his wife, saying, "A woodman
dreamt he had got a deer, but he did not know where it was.
Now I have got the deer; so his dream was a reality." "It is
you," replied his wife, "who have been dreaming you saw a
woodman. Did he get the deer? and is there really such a
person? It is you who have got the deer: how, then, can his
dream be a reality?" "It is true," assented the husband,
"that I have got the deer. It is therefore of little importance
whether the woodman dreamt the deer or I dreamt the
woodman."

Now when the woodman reached his home, he became
much annoyed at the loss of the deer; and in the night he
actually dreamt where the deer then was, and who had got
it. So next morning he proceeded to the place indicated in
his dream,—and there it was. He then took legal steps to
recover possession; and when the case came on, the magistrate delivered the following judgment:—"The plaintiff began with a real deer and an alleged dream. He now comes

forward with a real dream and an alleged deer. The defendant really got the deer which plaintiff said he dreamt, and is now trying to keep it; while, according to his wife, both the woodman and the deer are but the figments of a dream, so that no one got the deer at all. However, here is a deer, which you had better divide between you."

When the Prince of Cheng heard this story, he cried out, "The magistrate himself must have dreamt the case!" So he enquired of his prime minister, who replied, "Only the Yellow Emperor and Confucius could distinguish dream from reality, and they are unfortunately dead. I advise, therefore, that the magistrate's decision be confirmed."

Why Confucius was sad

Confucius was one day sitting at leisure, when Tzu Kung went in to attend upon him. The disciple noticed that his master wore a sorrwful air; but not venturing to ask the reason, went out and told Yen Hui. Thereupon Yen Hui seized his guitar and began to sing; at which Confucius called him in and said, "Hui, why are you alone glad?" "Master," retorted Hui, "why are you alone sorrowful?" "First answer my question," said Confucius. "I once heard you declare," explained Yen Hui, "that he who was contented with his lot and prepared for the appointments of destiny, could not be sorrowful. Accordingly, I am glad."

The master's expression for a moment changed. Then he answered, saying, "I did use those words. But you are misapplying them here. Such utterances are of the past. Rather adopt those which I deliver now. Alas! you know only the superficial principle that he who is contented with his lot and prepared for the appointments of destiny cannot be sorrowful. You do not perceive the deeper sorrow entailed by this very absence of sorrow. I will tell you all.

"You cultivate yourself. You accept success or failure as they may come. You see that life and death are independent of your efforts. You maintain your moral and mental equilibrium. And you consider that under such conditions of contentment and preparedness you are without sorrow.

"Now, I edited the *Odes* and the *Book of History*. I defined the functions of Music and Ceremonial. I did this in order to benefit the whole earth, and to be a guide for posterity. I did not do it merely for my own personal advantage, nor for that of my own individual State. But now, even in my own State, the obligations between prince and subject are forgotten; charity and duty to one's neighbor are passing away; and right feeling is all but gone. If then the truth cannot prevail for a brief space in a single State, how is it likely to prevail over the whole earth through all generations to come? I know now that all I have achieved is in vain; and I am utterly at a loss to discover the true remedy. Therefore I am sad."

Rest

Tzu Kung said to Confucius, "Master, I am aweary, and would fain have rest."

"In life," replied the sage, "there is no rest."

"Shall I, then, never have rest?" asked the disciple.

"You will," said Confucius. "Behold the tombs which lie around; some magnificent, some mean. In one of these you will find rest."

"How wonderful is Death!" rejoined Tzu Kung. "The wise man rests, the worldly man is engulfed therein."

"My son," said Confucius, "I see that you understand. Other men know life only as a boon: they do not perceive that it is a bane. They know old age as a state of weakness: they do not perceive that it is a state of ease. They know death only as an abomination: they do not perceive that it is a state of rest.

"How grand," cried Yen Tzu, "is the old conception of Death! The virtuous find rest, the wicked are engulfed therein. In death, each reverts to that from which he came. The ancients regarded death as a return to, and life as an absence from, home. And he who forgets his home becomes an outcast and a byword in his generation."

Cosmogony

Our Master Lieh Tzu dwelt on a vegetable plot in the Cheng State for forty years, and no man knew him for what he was. The Prince, his ministers, and all the state officials looked upon him as one of the common herd. A time of dearth fell upon the State, and he was preparing to migrate to Wei, when his disciples said to him: 'Now that our Master is going away without any prospect of returning, we have ventured to approach you, hoping for instruction. Are there no words from the lips of Hu-Ch'iu Tzu-lin that you can impart to us?' Lieh Tzu smiled and said: 'Do you suppose that Hu Tzu dealt in words? However, I will try to repeat to you what my Master said on one occasion to Po-hun Mou-jen.

I was standing by and heard his words, which ran as follows:—

"There is a Creative Principle which is itself uncreated; there is a Principle of Change which is itself unchanging. The Uncreated is able to create life; the Unchanging is able to effect change. That which is produced cannot but continue producing; that which is evolved cannot but continue evolving. Hence there is constant production and constant evolution. The law of constant production and of constant evolution at no time ceases to operate.

The commentator says: 'That which is once involved in the destiny of living things can never be annihilated.' So is it with the Yin and the Yang, so is it with the Four Seasons.[1] The Uncreated we may surmise to be Alone in itself.

'The Supreme, the Non-Engendered—how can its reality be proved? We can only suppose that it is mysteriously One, without beginning and without end.' The Unchanging goes to and fro, and its range is illimitable. We may surmise that it stands Alone, and that its Ways are inexhaustible."

---

[1] The Yin and the Yang are the positive and negative principles of nature, alternately predominating in day and night.

'In the Book of the Yellow Emperor it is written: "The Spirit of the Valley dies not; it may be called the Mysterious Feminine. The issuing-point of the Mysterious Feminine must be regarded as the Root of the Universe. Subsisting to all eternity, it uses its force without effort."

'That, then, which engenerds all things is itself unengendered; that by which all things are evolved is itself untouched by evolution. Self-engendered and self-evolved, it has in itself the elements of substance, appearance, wisdom, strength, dispersion and cessation. Yet it would be a mistake to call it by any one of these names.'

Causality

In the course of Lich Tzu's instruction by HHu-ch'iu Tzu-lin, the latter said to him: 'You must familiarize yourself with the theory of consequents before you can talk of regulating conduct.' Lieh Tzu said: 'Will you explain what you mean by the theory of consequents?' 'Look at your shadow,' said his Master, 'and then you will know.' Lieh turned and looked at his shadow. When his body was bent, the shadow was crooked; when his body was upright,the shadow was straight. Thus it appeared that the attributes of straightness and crookedness were not inherent in the shadow, but corresponeded to certain positions of the body. Likewise, contraction and extension are not inherent in the subject, but take place in obedience to external causes. Holding this theory of consequents is to be at home in the antecedent.

Kuan Yin spoke to the Master Lieh Tzu, saying: 'If speech is sweet, the echo will be sweet; if speech is harsh, the echo will be harsh. If the body is long, the shadow will be long; if the body is short, the shadow will be short, Reputation is like an echo, personal experiences like a shadow.

'Hence the saying: "Heed your words, and they will meet with harmonious response; heed your actions and they will find agreeable accord." Therefore, the sage observes the origin in order to know the issue, scrutinizes the past in order to know the future. Such is the principle wherby he attains foreknowledge.

'The standard of conduct lies with one's own self; the testing of it lies with other men. We are impelled to love those who love us, and to hate those who hate us. T'ang and Wu loved the Empire, and therefore each became king. Chieh and Chou hated the Empire, and herefore they perished. Here we have the test applied. He who does not follow Tao when standard and test are both clear may be likened to one who, when leaving a house, does not go by the door, or, when travelling abroad, does not keep to the straight road. To seek profit in this way is surely impossible.

'You may consider the virtues of Shen Nung and Yu Yen, you may examine the books of Yu, Hsia, Shang and Chou, you may weigh the utterances of great teachers and sages, but will find no instance of preservation or destruction, fullness or decay, which has not obeyed this supreme Law.'

Effort and Destiny

Effort said to Destiny:

'Your achievements are not equal to mine.' 'Pray what do you achieve in the working of things,' replied Destiny, 'that you would compare yourself with me?' 'Why,' said Effort, 'the length of man's life, his measure of success, his rank, and his wealth, are all things which I have the power to determine.' To this, Destiny made reply: 'P'eng Tsu's wisdom did not exceed that of Yao and Shun, yet he lived to the age of eight hundred. Yen Yüan's ability was not inferior to that of the average man, yet he died at the early age of thirty-two. The virtue of Confucius was not less than that of the feudal princes, yet he was reduced to sore straits between Ch'en and Ts'ai. The conduct of Chou, of the Yin dynasty, did not surpass that of the Three Men of Virtue, yet he occupied a kingly throne.

Chi Cha would not accept the overlordship of Wu, while T'ien Heng usurped sole power in Ch'i. Po I and Shu Ch'i starved to death at Shou-yang, while Chi Shih waxed rich at Chan-ch'in. If these results were compassed by your efforts, how is it that you allotted long life to P'eng Tsu and and untimely death to Yen Yüan; that you awarded discomfiture to the sage and success to the impious, humiliation to the wise man and high honors to the fool, poverty to the good and wealth to the wicked?' 'If, as you say,' rejoined Effort, 'I have really no control over events, it is not, then, owing to *your* management that things turn out as they do?' Destiny replied: 'The very name "Destiny" shows that there can be no question of management in the case. When the way is straight, I push on; when it is crooked, I put up with it. Old age and early death, failure and success, high rank and hamble station, riches and poverty—all these come naturally and of themselves. How can I know anything about them?'

🈐

On one hand, there is life, and on the other, ther is that which produces life; there is form, nd there is that which imparts form; there is sound,and there is that which causes sound; there is color, and there is that which causes color; there is tatse, and there is that which causes taste.

Things that have been endowed with life die; but that which produces life itself never comes to an end. The origin of orm is matter; but that which imparts form has no material existence. The genesis of sound lies in the sense of hearing; but that which causes sound is never audible to the ear. The source of color is vision; but that which produces color never manifests itself to the eye. The origin of taste lies in the palate; but that which causes taste is never perceived by that sense. All these phenomena are functions of the principle of Inaction.[1]

To be at will either bright or obscure, soft or hard, short or long, round or square, alive or dead, hot or cold, buoyant

[1] *Wu—wei*, Inaction, here stands for the inert, unchanging Tao.

or sinking, treble or bass, present or absent, black or white, sweet or bitter, fetid or fragrant:—this it is to be devoid of knowledge, yet all-knowing, destitute of power, yet all-powerful.

On his journey to Wei, the Master Lieh Tzu took a meal by the roadside. His followers espied an old skull, and pulled aside the undergrowth to show it to him. Turning to his disciple Po Feng, the Master said: 'That skull and I both know that there is no such thing as absolute life or death.

'If we regard ourselves as apssing along the road of evolution, then I am alive and he is dead. But looked at from the standpoint of the Absolute, since there is no such principle as life in itself, it follows that there can be no such thing as death.'

This knowledge is better than all your methods of prolonging life, a more potent source of happiness than any other.'

In the Book of the Yellow Emperor it is written: 'When form becomes active it produces not form but shadow; when sound becomes active it produces not sound but echo.'

When Not-Being becomes active, it does not produce Not-Being but Being. Form is something that must come to an end. Heaven and earth, then, have an end, even as we all have an end. But whether the end is complete we do not know.

'When there is conglomeration, form comes into being; when there is dispersion, it comes to an end. That is what we mortals mean by beginning and end. But although for us, in a state of conglomeration, this condensation into form constitutes a beginning, and its dispersion an end, from the standpoint of dispersion, it is void and calm that constitute the beginning, and condensation into form the end. Hence there is perpetual alternation in what constitutes beginning and end, and the underlying Truth is that there is neither any beginning nor any end at all.'

The course of evolution ends where it started, without a beginning; it finishes up where ir began, in Not-Being. That which has life returns again into the Lifeless; that which has form returns again into the formless. This, that I call the Lifeless, is not the original Lifelessness. This, that I call the formless, is not the original Formlessness.

'That which is here termed the Lifeless has formerly possessed life, and subsequently passed into the extinction of death, whereas the original Lifelessness from the beginning knows neither life nor extinction.'[1]

That which has life must by the law of its being come to an end; and the end can no more be avoided than the living creature can help having been born. So thathe who hopes to perpetuate his life or to shut out death is deceived as to his destiny.

The spiritual element in man is allotted to him by Heaven, his corporeal frame by earth. The part that belongs to Heaven is ethereal and dispersive, the part that belongs to earth is dense and dendind to conglomeration. When the spirit parts from the body, each of these elements resumes it sture nature. That is why disembodied spirits are called *kuei*, which means 'returning', that is, returning to their true dwelling-place.

Yen Tzu said: 'How excellent was the ancients' view of death!—bringing rest to the good and subjection to the wicked. Death is the boundary-line of virtue.[2]

'The ancients spoke of the dead as *kuei-jen* (men who have returned). But if the dead are men who have returned, the living are men on a journey. Those who are on a journey and think not of returning have cut themselves off from

[1] We have here again the distinction between the unchanging life-giving Principle (Tao), which is itself without life, and the living things themselves, which are in a perpetual flux between life and death.

[2] That is, Death abolishes all artificial and temporary distinctions between good and evil, which only hold good in this world of relativity.

their home. Should any one man cut himself off from his home, he would incur universal reprobation. But all mankind being homeless, there is none to see the error. Imagine one who leaves his native village, separates himself from all his kith and kin, dissipates his patrimony and wanders away to the four corners of the earth, never to return:—what manner of man is this? The world will surely set him down as a profligate and a vagabond. On the other hand, imagine onw who clings to respectability and the things of this life, holds cleverness and capacity in high esteem, builds himself up a reputation, and plays the braggart amongst his fellow men without knowing where to stop:—what manner of man, once more, is this? The world will surely look upon him as a gentleman of great wisdom and counsel. Both of these men have lost their way, yet the world will consort with the one, and not with theother. Only the Sage knows with whom to consort and from whom to hold aloof.'

'He consorts with those who regard life and death merely as waking ans sleeping, and holds aloof from those who are steeped in forgetfulness of their return.'

Mr. Kuo of the Ch'i State was very rich, while Mr. Hsiang of ths Sung State was very poor. The latter travelled from Sung to Ch'i and asked the other for the secret of his prosperity. Mr. Kuo told him. "It is because I am a good thief," he said. "The first year I began to be a thief, I had just enough. The second year, I had ample. The third year, I reaped a great harvest. And, in course of time, I found myself the owner of whole villages and districts.' Mr. Hsiang was overjoyed; he understood the word "thief" in its literal sense, but he did not understand the true way of becoming a thief. Accordingly, he climbed over walls and broke into houses, grabbing everything he could see or lay hands upon. But before very long his thefts brought him into trouble, and he was stripped even of what he had previously possessed. Thinking that Mr. Kuo has basely deceived him, Hsiang went to him with a bitter complaint. "Tell me," said Mr. Kuo, "how did you set about being a thief?" On learning from Mr. Hsiang what had happened, he cried out: "Alas and alack! You have been brought to this pass because you went the wrong way to work. Now let me put you on the right track. We all know that heaven has its seasons, and that earth has its riches. Well, the things that I steal are the riches of heaven and earth, each in their season—the fertilizing rain-water from the clouds, and the natural products of mountain and meadow-land. Thus I grow my grain and ripen my corps, build my walls and construct my tenements. From the dry land I steal winged and four-footed game, from the rivers I steal fish and turtles. There is nothing that I do not steal. For corn and grain, clay and wood, birds and beasts, fishes and turtles are all products of nature. How can I claim them as mine?

"Yet, stealing in this way from nature, I bring on myself no retribution. But gold, jade, and precious stones, stores of grain, silk stuffs, and other kinds of property, are things accumulated by men, not bestowed upon us by nature. So who can complain if he gets into trouble by stealing them?"

Mr. Hsiang, in a state of great preplexity, and fearing to be led astray a second time by Mr. Kuo, went off to consult Tung Kuo, a man of learning. Tung Kuo said to him: "Are you not already a thief in respect of your own body? You are stealing the harmony of the Yin and the Yang in order to keep alive and to maintain your bodily form. How much more, then, are you a thief with regard to external possessions! Assuredly, heaven and earth cannot be dissociated from the myriad objects of nature. To claim any one of these as your own betokens confusion of thought. Mr. Kuo's thefts are carried out in a spirit of justice, and therefore bring no retribuition. But your thefts were carried out in a spirit of self-seeking and therefore landed you in trouble. Those who take possession of property, whether public or private, are thieves.[1]

"Those who abstain from taking property, public or private, are also thieves.

'For no one can help possessing a body, and no one can help acquiring some property or other which cannot be got rid of with the best will in the world. Such thefts are unconscious thefts.'

The great principle of heaven and earth is to treat public property as such and private property as such. Knowing this principle, which of us is a thief, and at the same time which of us is not a thief?"[2]

[1] By 'taking possession of public property', as we have seen, Lieh Tzu means utilizing the products of Nature open to all—rain and the like.

[2] The object of this anecdote is to impress us with the unreality of mundane distinctions. Lieh Tzu is not much interested in the social aspect of the question. He is not an advocate of communism, nor does he rebel against the common-sense view that theft is a crime which must be punished. With him, everything is intended to lead up to the metaphysical standpoint.

Writings from Huai Nan Tzu

Life and Soul

There is mutual correspondence in the fluxes of nature. Creation is governed by unity. When this unity is comprehended there is nothing which is not apprehended. But through ignorance of this universal unity (The Tao) it is not possible to know any one thing.[1] For example, I am placed in the world and count also as a unit in it. May it not be that creation must have me to make it complete; would it be perfect without me? Nevertheless, I am a parcel of matter and creation is matter and I am matter. Why name each and other? We are all one matter. Nevertheless, is life, given me by Heaven, of any worth that it adds to the value of creation or would my annihilation be any injury to it? Further, since the Creator made me an ignorant clod, i.e., a man, I must submit to its decrees. How then may it be said that the invalid who seeks a leach, desiring to prolong his life, is not mistaken? How may it be sure that the man who seeks death by suicide is not happy in his attempt? It may be that life will be but slavery and death would be a rest and surcease from toils. Life is but a vague mystery (vast wilderness). Who knows what is sginifies? Shall the Creator be asked not give life? Shall he be asked not give death? Desiring life yet not striving for it, disliking death and yet not refusing it. If my condition in life is humble, I will not despise it; if honorable, yet I will not rejoice. Waiting on the times of heaven (or nature) the *True Man* does not rush to prolong

[1] The first unity is Tao and the second is the unity of *wu*, or things. The relative value of life's parts can only be truly valued by the Tao. The Tao is head and source of all, and ignorance of it implies one knows nothing.

life. In life I have a seven-foot body, in death I have a coffin length of soil. As a living being, I add one to the kind of those who have form: just as, in death, I sink into the formless kind. Thus the sum of matter is not increased by my living: even the thickness of the soil is not swelled by my death. How then should I feel the joy of life or sorrow of death, the gain of one or loss of the other?

Again, the Creator's molding and guidance of matter may be illustrated by the potter's kneading of clay. He takes it from the soil, and having made it into a bason or dish, it is still not different from what it was in the soil, since, when the vessel is broken, it gets dispersed and returns again to its source: and in this state it is in no wise different in nature from a plate or bason as made. The people who live in villages bordering on the river lead its waters to irrigate their gardens, to which the water has no objection. The poor people disgusted with the filthy pools around drain them into the flowing river, but the foul water feels no exhilaration. Therefore, there is no difference whether the water is in the river or irrigating the garden: it is a matter of indifference to the water whether it lies in the filthy pool or in the flowing Chiang.[1] Therefore the sage rests satisfied with his position, whether high or low, and joyfully follows his work and avocation of sage.

Grief and joy are aberrations from virtue (teh): pleasure and anger are the excesses of man trying to follow Tao: love and hate are the exasperations of the mind. Therefore the saying, "life is as the change of the seasons: death is as the flux of matter." Immobile, it is inactive with Yin (negative, all avenues are closed up): mobile, it is active with Yang, (positive, all avenues open out). The spirit begins pure, unadulterated, with a fund of tranquility, and undisturbed by the friction of life, has the world at his feet in virtue. The heart is the master of the physical body and the spirit is the

---

[1] The cultured man should not dislike death since it means only a return to original nature by dissolution. Here there is another insight into the trend of thought under stress of danger and anarchy.

pearl of the heart. When the body travails without rest there
ensues a collapse: when the spirit is ceaselessly used exhaustion will follow. Hence the sage esteems and respects the
body and the spirit and dares not abuse them. Think of the
semi-circular seal of jade belonging to Hsia Hou's family.[1]
It was locked in a box and put in a safe because it was most
precious. But how precious the spirit! It is to be prized even
more than the seal of Hou-Hsia. Therefore, the sage re-
sponding to everything with an unbiased mind, with a mind
free from prepossession, he approaches all facts, and must
investigate the law that governs them. Spending his life in
the spirit of sweet reasonableness, unmoved by sensuous
desire, necessarily he looks thoroughly into the economy of
things and so completes his life in peaceful happiness.
Hence he does not separate himself very much from the one
nor is attached overmuch to the other.[2] He cherishes virtue,
and he warms himself at thefires of harmony that he may
be in line with heaven. He is in agreement with the Tao; he
is neighbor of virtue. He does not put happiness first nor is
he the first to create distress. The aura and soul are domi-
ciled in his home, (the body), and the Spirit guards the vital
root. Death and life make no difference to him. So the name
"Most Spiritual."

He who is named the True Man, implies an identity of
his nature with the Tao. Thoroughly equipped he yet gives
the appearance of having nothing, (like an immortal). Reality is he, yet he gives the appearance of being witless. He
stands on the one thing (the Tao) with undivided attention
and has no second thing in mind: he enriches his inner life
without being governed by the affections, such as *like* and
dislike.[3] Conscious of the primordial simplicity of being, he

[1]The seal of Hou Hsia is a precious jade of the Hsia dynasty (2183-1752
B.C.?), cut in half a circle. The half circle symbolizes winter—and in winter
the earth is in lethargy, so heaven alone is active.

[2]This is different from the *nil admirari* state of mind. For here there
is an admiration of the Tao which should be seen from the perspective of
the next sentence, "He cherishes virtue and warms himself. . . ."

[3]When the inner life is under perfect control, love and hate, like and
dislike, do not move the sage or True Man.

does not strive (for the decorations of an outward culture)
but reverts to (pristine and unadultered) simplicity. He is
concerned with foundations, he protects the spirit that he
may soar to the circumference of the universe. Far and wide,
at pleasure, (or following his own volition) he soars beyond
this "world of dirt": and suspires in the sphere of *wu wei*,
spirit-action. How vast and wide his attainments! He harbors no scheme of cunning in his heart: hence life and death
are both great and dignified: they are alike. Though the
firmament covers and the earth sustains all, yet he is not tied
to them (but maintains an independency): the spirit is above
the fluxes. True in his judgments, free from defects, by
which evil could enter, he has no controversies with life.
Though the world is empirical, and tries this and that
method, one essays this another that, but he sticks to principles. Such an one as this is verily in harmony with his being,
depending not on the sight of the eye or the hearing of the
ear or on courage, he has his heart and purpose governed by
the spirit within. The will is concentrated on the inner life:
he is permeated with and a partner of the Tao-Unity. He
lives in a state of unconsciousness of his actions, he is una-
ware of whither he goes: i.e., he is not uncertain how to act,
the spirit is clear and will guide action unerringly. He comes
and goes as it were mechanically and his actions are
prompt.[1] There is no physically prompted action, the heart
is as dead ashes. All material things are as nothing. Without
learning he knows; without seeing he sees; without doing he
achieves: without immediate study he can discuss; he responds to influence there is a flash as from light and a
shadow as of substance.[2] With the Tao as the rule of life,
he waits, in this spirit, on every thing, in secret. He preserves
the foundation of the Great Purity entertaining none of the

[1]These last two sentences describe the man whose mind is completely
under the sway of the spirit and not concerned with worldliness. There is
"guidance" because of this and his emptiness is filled.

[2]Divine inspiration, in western terms, would be the parallel for this
state.

appetites: matter in no way seduces him. He is impervious to the sway of the senses and free from anxieties. Were you to heat a great lake of water it wuldn't make him feel hot: if you were to freeze the rivers, he wouldn't feel their cold: if the thunderstorm sundered the mountains, he wouldn't be frightened: if raging tornadoes obscured the day he wouldn't be perturbed. Such is the man whose heart is fixed on the Tao. The senses have no power to disturb him. Hence the sight of a precious jade or jewel affects him no more than an ordinary stone. An interview with the emperor does not flurry him more than the visit of an ordinary guest. A sight of the two beauties Mao Ch'iang and Hsi Shih stirs him no more than a sight of an ugly person would.

Death and life are looked on as but a transformation: the myriad creation is all of a kind, there is a kinship through all. Being one in essence with the fundamental of the Great Purity he moves in the realm of the formless. He does not pollute the essence, nor abuse the spirit, i.e., he does not sully the pristine element of life nor waste the energies of the spirit. The soul is a living part of a whole universe, and is placed in an environment of great clarity. Therefore he does not dream during his sleep: the intelligence is not dimmed; the spirit maintaining its own uinty, his knowledge is not mixed with scheming concepts. The animal spirits are not depressed nor is the spirit too buoyant. His activities and movements, from first to last, are of a homogeniety. Closing the eyes on the world of sense, he lives in the abstruse realms of the Tao, yet he sees as though he were in a house full of light. Reposing in this ideal realm (not in the crooked ways of schemes) he takes his flight into regions of formless space. Living in regions that could not be visualized, roaming without a fixed location, his movements have no vestiges, his tranquility no substance. In being, he is as one lost, living, he is as one dead: he can go in and out through the impenetrable; the ghosts of the dead and of the divinities are his ministers. He probes into the unfathomable, he penetrates into the unspatial since the Tao transmits the varied forms.

The beginning and end are as a circle, so others can't find the truth. *This is the wherefore of the spirit. All life hangs together in the Tao.* This spirituality mounts aloft to the Tao. This is the peregrination of the Perfect Man. As to such motions as breathing and blowing, inhaling and exhaling, spitting out the old, drawing in the new breath, imitating in gymnastic the steps of the bear, the fluttering and expanding of the wings of birds, the ablutions of the duck, the stooping of the gibbon, the glare of the owl, the concentrated stare of the tiger,—these motions are the means used by man to cultivate the bodily form.[1] The Perfect Man does not bother his mind about them. They are those things that disarrange and confuse the mind. When the spirit in its peregrinations does not lose its abundance of life, and when it never deteriorates it will ever have the everlasting vernal vivifications of matter. In this unison with the *Tao*, the sesasonable transformations take place in the heart. Without disorder of time, or detriment to matter there is ample benevolence. Moreover should some disability or disease strike the bodily frame, or should it undergo change this would in no wise harm the spirit. Should the earthly tenement fail the spirit is in no way destroyed. Should a man be leprous, for instance, he still can walk and the purpose of the mind is in no wise changed, during life. Should a person, on the other hand, be seized with madness, his physical form is not despoiled, but the spirit is about to take its flight and pass beyond its bounds. No one can ever say what a madman will do next. Though the form dies the spirit does not die, because that which can undergo no change supplies and respomds to that which is subject to change, and to the

---

[1]The Taoist does not believe in physical indulgences and is concerned with the body only as the medium of the spirit. In this sense Taoism is closer to the New Testament than the Old, where the physical body is seen as the seat of weakness. In the New Testament the physical body is seen as the residence of the spirit (II Corinthians, 5:1), or as the "temple" of the spirit (I Corinthians, 6:19): "Know ye not that your body is the temple of the Holy Ghost *which is* in you, which ye have of God . . ."

myriad fluctuations and thousand changes which never come to an end. That which is subject to death reverts, in turn, to the formless. That which does not change lives on with heaven and earth. Wood dies because the sap has left it. But can wood give life to itself? That which gives body to the form is not the form itself: (it is *Ch'i*, vitalism.) The Giver of life has never died, but that which it begets is subject to death. That which causes the flux of matter (Tao) does not undergo the flux, but what it changes undergoes the change. He who makes light of the world or thinks little of empire, has an undivided heart and an untroubled spirit. He looks on death and life as being of a piece. Viewing life as a minor affair, he has no fears. Cognizant of the flux of life, the understanding is free from perplexity and void of doubts. Seeing that the multitude looks on this doctrine as so many idle words let me give a few examples to substantiate it.

The reason why people think it a matter of joy to be masters of men is that these have all that the senses can desire, and can command all those luxuries that minister to the comfort of the person. Lofty fabrics and storied palaces people affect and covet: yet Yao did not decorate his house, nor carve and paint his palace columns. Rare delicacies of unusual taste are things people like but Yao lived on the simplest fare and the plainest soups. Embroidered white fox furs are what people covet, but Yao covered his person with the plainest calico, and a deer skin fended off the cold. He did not regale himself with luxuries more than others, but he superimposed the anxieties of office on himself. Hence in transferring the empire to Shun, the act was not simply a matter of renunciation, but truly a release from burden. This was really to think little of the glories of empire.

Yü travelled south inspecting the empire, and when crossing the river a yellow dragon shouldered the boat. The boatmen changed colour, but Yü, smiling genially said, "I'm doing my utmost in the interest of the people, discharging my duties in obedience to heaven. Living, I'm but a guest, dying I return home. Why should we be disturbed in our peace? The sight of a dragon is no more than a lizard." Since he didn't turn color, the dragon pressed his ears and dropping his tail departed. Yü thought it a little matter to see monstrous animals.

A ghost-like witch of Cheng, telling the fortune of Hu Tzu Lin, though he couldn't live long, and mentioned the fact to Lieh Tzu. Lieh Tzu went weeping to tell Hu Tzu. Hu Tzu replied "I hold that our spiritual nature comes from heaven, and our physical frame from the earth. Honors and wealth are not lasting, death comes on apace." Thus we see that Hu Tzu looked on life and death as being but the same thing.

Tzu Ch'iu when he was 54 years of age had an illness which left his body deformed. The nape of his neck was higher than his head, his jaw was bent to his chest, his lips were distorted and his head was twisted. He crawled one day to a well and seeing his reflection in the water, exclaimed: "How wonderful! Great is the work of the Creator, who hath fashioned me in this goodly way!" The change did not disfigure the real form, in his view.

We may, therefore, deduce that in Yao's view of life, the empire, or being an emperor, was of no great consequence. Considering Yü's mind it is clear that he thought empire was a paltry affair. Probing Hu Tzu's disquisition we can see that life and death are but two phases of the same thing, in his estimation. From the action of Tzu Ch'iu we know that the fluxes of life are governed by identical laws.

Now the Perfect Man[1] leans on a support that cannot be uprooted and travels on an unobstructed road.[2] He is en-

---

[1]There are three kinds of "perfect men" in Taoism: The Sage, the True Man, and the Perfect Man. They have attained a pefection of character through suppression of desire and worldliness; But beyond this they have found *Tao*, an identity with the cosmic spirit. The Taoist idea is not so different here from the Christian Saint who is "God intoxicated," as Spinoza called it. Here we have the "Tao-filled" man.

[2]There are no closed avenues to the God-intoxicated or Tao-filled sage.

dowed with an inexhaustible store of spiritual goods and instructed in the methods of *"no-death"*:[1] none of his journeys are unsuccessful: there is no avenue not open to him. Life does not clog his mind, nor death cloud his spirit. He guards the heavenly dispensation in all his activities without departing from its behests. Adversity and happiness, loss and gain, the thousand changes and myriad fluxes of life fail to worry him. A man of this calibre preserves his pristine spirit, and upholds his mind. Like the cicada and snake he can throw off his mortal coil and wander in the great Empyrean. With light or airy step and with the greatest ease he swiftly enters the sable heaven (out of sight). Even the phoenix cannot keep him company in pace, much less the (fabulous) Ch'ih Yen. How can power, emoluments, or position influence or shrivel such a mind. When Yen was near death, he refused to break his faith by entering into a treaty with Ts'ui Chu, the traitorous minister, who designed to slay the king. The threats of Ts'ui failed to shake Yen tzu's loyalty. Chih Hua did not fear death in battle, and so the Prince of Lu vainly tempted him with a great bribe to stay out of battle. Hence we gather that Yen Tzu could act under the compulsion of goodness, but could not be frightened by military force. Chih Hua could be arrested in his course by the power of right could not be moved by gain. The superior man will die for right, but he cannot be detained by the thoughts of honors and gain. He was determined to do the right and could not be disturbed by fear of death.

These men, then, had in view nothing but righteousness. They were not hampered by material things. How much less so can worldly allurements deceive the *Man of Wu–wei*, of spirit-action. Yao looked not on the empire as a thing of honour (to cling to): he therefore handed it to Shun. Kung

---

[1]Taoists believe that there are two deaths—one of the body and one of the soul or spirit. "No-death" of the body is used to lead men on to think of the eternal life of the soul. When a man has the two, his spirit preserves unity after death and is not dispersed into seven parts as is commonly believed. No-death refers to this condition, where unity is preserved.

Tzu Cha conceded the throne, as he did not consider it the chief honor of life. Tzu Kan did not look on the possession of the jade to be true riches, so refused the throne—the precious jade. Wu Kuang would not injure righteousness by living, so he threw himself into the whirling pool (and died).

From these instances it is clear that the highest honor is not that pertaining to official position: the greatest wealth is not that which comes from worldly riches. The empire is the very greatest thing in the world, yet this has been relinquished (by Yao) to another. There is nothing dearer to a man than his body, but it was thrown into the whirlpool. Having said this the last word is said. These are the greatest things, and in saying this all is said.

These instances refer to people who have not been entangled by the world,—men with spirits free from the glamor of life who do not look upon a throne as a thing of honor to be coveted. Thinking of these men that stand right above us, and considering their view of life, probing their profound meaning of Tao and its works of virtue, we cannot but blush as we look on the conventional life we live.

Part 3
CH'AN AND CHINESE BUDDHISM

CHINESE
BUDDHISM
    The Sutra of Forty-two Sections
    Selections from the Surangama Sutra

CH'AN
BUDDHISM
    On Trust in the Heart
    From the Conversations of Shen-hui
    Selections from the Platform Sutra of Hui-neng

The Sutra of
Forty-two Sections

Having attained Buddhahood, the World-honored One thought thus: "To be free from the passions and to be calm, this is the most excellent Way."

He was absorbed in Great Meditation, subdued all evil ones, and in Deer Park[1] caused to revolve the Wheel of Dharma, which was the Fourfold Truth,[2] and converted the five Bhikshus,[3] Kaudinya, etc., inducing them to attain Enlightenment.

Again, there were other Bhikshus who implored the Buddha to remove their doubts which they had concerning his doctrine. The World-honored One illumined all their minds through his authoritative teachings. The Bhikshus, joining their hands and reverentially bowing, followed his august instructions.

(1) The Buddha said: "Those who leave their parents, go out of the home, understand the mind, reach the source,

[1]Deer Park refers to a Buddhist legend where a Bodhisattva saved a herd of deer from being slaughtered by a royal hunting party. It is said that the Deer Park, which is in Benares, was the place where Buddha "first caused the Wheel of the Good Law to revolve." The story of Deer Park, along with other lectures and anecdotes, can be found in D.T. Suzuki's *Sermons of a Buddhist Abbot*, (the most available edition is published by Samuel Weiser, Inc., New York, 1971), from which this complete translation of the "Sutra of Forty-two Sections" was taken.

[2]The Buddha's Fourfold Noble Truth is that Life is suffering, ignorance is the cause of suffering, Nirvana is the goal of life and transcends pain and pleasure, and to reach such enlightenment moral laws must be put into practice.

[3]Bhikshus means literally "beggars," and is a term used to stand for Buddhist monks.

and comprehend the immaterial, are called Shaman.[1]

"Those who observe the two hundred and fifty precepts[2] of morality, who are pure and spotless in their behavior, and who exert themselves for the attainment of the four fruits of saintship, are called Arhats.

"The Arhat is able to fly through space and assume different forms; his life is eternal, and there are times when he causes heaven and earth to quake.

"Next is the Anagamin. At the end of his life, the spirit of the Anagamin ascends to the nineteenth heaven and obtains Arhatship.

"Next is the Skridagamin. Ths Skridagamin ascends to the heavens [after his death], comes back to the earth once more, and then attains Arhatship.

"Next is the Srotaapanna. The Srotaapanna dies seven times and is born seven times, when he finally attains Arhatship.[3]

"By the severance of the passions is meant that like the limbs severed they are never again made use of."(2) The Buddha said: "The homeless Shaman cuts off the passions, frees himself of attachments, understands the source of his own mind, penetrates the deepest doctrine of Buddha, and comprehends the Dharma which is immaterial. He has no prejudice in his heart, he has nothing to hanker after. He is not hampered by the thought of the Way, nor is he entangled in karma. No prejudice, no compulsion, no discipline, no enlightenment, and no going up through the grades, and yet in possession of all honors in itself,—this is called the Way."

[1]For the sake of clarity I have incorporated some of the references of Samuel Beal's translation. For example, Suzuki translates the word "Shaman" (which Beal uses) as Çramana, from the root çram, "to exert oneself," or "to make an effort."

[2]These can be found in the *Sacred Books of the East* series, Vols. XIII, XVII, XX, under the Vinaya texts.

[3]These three designations, the Anagamin, the Skridagamin, and the Srotaapanna mean, respectively, "one who never returns"; "one who comes back"; and "one who gets in the stream."

(3) The Buddha said: "Those who shaving their heads and faces become Shaman and who receive instruction in the Way, should surrender all worldly possessions and be contented with whatever they obtain by begging. One meal a day and one lodging under a tree, and neither should be repeated. For what makes one stupid and irrational is attachments and the passions."

(4) The Buddha said: "There are ten things considered good by all beings, and ten things evil. What are they? Three of them depend upon the body, four upon the mouth, and three upon thought.

"Three evil deeds depending upon the body are: killing, stealing, and committing adultery. The four depending upon the mouth are: slandering, cursing, lying, and flattery. The three depending upon thought are: envy, anger, and infatuation. All these things are against the Holy Way, and therefore they are evil.

"When these evils are not done, there are ten good deeds."

(5) The Buddha said: "If a man who has committed many a misdemeanor does not repent and cleanse his heart of the evil, retribution will come upon his person as sure as the streams run into the ocean which becomes ever deeper and wider.

"If a man who has committed a misdemeanor come to the knowledge of it, reform himself, and practice goodness, the force of retribution will gradually exhaust itself as a disease gradually loses its baneful influence when the patient perspires."

(6) The Buddha said: "When an evil-doer, seeing you practice goodness, comes and maliciously insults you, you should patiently endure it and not feel angry with him, for the evil-doer is insulting himself by trying to insult you."

(7) The Buddha said: "Once a man came unto me and denounced me on account of my observing the Way and practicing great loving-kindness. But I kept silent and not answer him. The denunciation ceased. I then asked him, 'If

you bring a present to your neighbor and he accepts it not, does the present come back to you?' The man replied, 'It will.' I said, 'You denounce me now, but as I accept it not, you must take the worng deed back on your own person. it is like echo succeeding sound, it is like shadow following object; you never escape the effect of your own evil deeds. Be therefore mindful, and cease from doing evil.' "

(8) The Buddha said: "Evil-doers who denounce the wise resemble a person who spits against the sky; the spittle will never reach the sky, but comes down on himself. Evil-doers again resemble a man who stirs the dust against the wind; the dust is never raised without doing him injury. Thus, the wise will never be hurt, but the curse is sure to destroy the evil-doers themselves."

(9) The Buddha said: "If you endeavor to embrace the Way through much learning, the Way will not be understood. If you observe the Way with simplicity of heart, great indeed is this Way."

(10)[1] The Buddha said: "Those who rejoice in seeing others observe the Way will obtain great blessing." A Shaman asked the Buddha, "Would this blessing ever be destroyed?" The Buddha said, "It is like a lighted torch whose flame can be distributed to ever so many other torches which people may bring along; and therewith they will cook food and dispel darkness, while the original torch itself remains burning ever the same It is even so with the bliss of the Way."

(11) The Buddha said: "It is better to feed one good man than to feed one hundred bad men. It is better to feed one who observes the five precepts of Buddha than to feed on thousand good men. It is better to feed one Srotaapanna than to feed ten thousands of those who observe the five precepts of Buddha. It is better to feed one Skridagamin

[1]Starting with this paragraph Suzuki's numbering of the forty-two sections is somewhat different from other translations. Samuel Beal, for example, incorporates Suzuki's 10th section into his 9th, and begins the 10th section with the paragraph on feeding (Suzuki's 11th).

than to feed one million of Srotaapannas. It is better to feed one Anagamin than to feed ten millons of Skridagamins. It is better to feed one Arhat than to feed one hundred millions of Anagamins. It is better to feed one Pratyekabuddha than to feed one billion of Arhats. It is better to feed one of the Buddhas, either of the present, or of the past, or of the buture, than to feed ten billions of Pratyekabuddhas. It is better to feed one who is above knowledge, one-sidedness, discipline, and enlightenment than to feed one hundred billions of Buddhas of the past, present, or future."

(12) The Buddha said: "There are twenty difficult things to attain [or to accomplish] in this world: (1) It is difficult for the poor to practice charity; (2) It is difficult for the strong and rich to observe the Way;[1] (3) It is difficult to disregard life and go to certain death; (4) It is only a favored few that get acquainted with a Buddhist sutra; (5) It is by rare opportunity that a person is born in the age of Buddha; (6) It is difficult to conquer the passions, to suppress selfish desires; (7) It is difficult not to hanker after that which is agreeable; (8) It is difficult not to get into a passion when slighted; (9) It is difficult not to abuse one's authority; (10) It is difficult to be even-minded and simple-hearted in all one's dealings with others; (11) It is difficult to be thorough in learning and exhaustive in investigation; (12) It is difficult to subdue selfish pride; (13) It is difficult not to feel contempt toward the unlearned; (14) It is difficult to be one in knowledge and practice; (15) It is difficult not to express an opinion about others;[2] (16) It is by rare opportunity that one is introduced to a true spiritual teacher; (17) It is difficult to gain an insight into the nature of being and to practice the Way; (18) It is difficult to follow the steps of a savior; (19) It is difficult to be always the master of oneself; (20) It

---

[1]Compare Matthew 19:24. "It is easier for a camel to go through the eye of a needle, than for a rich man to enter into the kingdom of God."

[2]Again, compare Matthew 7:1-2. "Judge not, that ye be not judged. For with what judgment ye judge, ye shall be judged."

is difficult to understand thoroughly the Ways of Buddha."

(13) A monk asked the Buddha: "Under what conditions is it possible to come to the knowledge of the past and to understand the most supreme Way?" The Buddha said: "Those who are pure in heart and single in purpose are able to understand the most supreme Way. It is like polishing a mirror, which becomes bright when the dust is removed. Remove your passions, and have no hankering, and the past will be revealed unto you."

(14) A monk asked the Buddha: "What is good, and what is great?" The Buddha answered: "Good is to practice the Way and to follow the truth. Great is the heart that is in accord with the Way."

(15) A monk asked the Buddha: "What is most powerful, and what is most illuminating?" The Buddha said: "Meekness is most powerful, for it harbors no evil thoughts, and, moreover, it is restful and full of strength. As it is free from evils, it is sure to be honored by all.[1]

"The most illuminating is a mind which is thoroughly cleansed of dirt,[2] and which, remaining pure, retains no blemishes. From the time when there was yet no heaven and earth till the present day, there is nothing in the ten quarters which is not seen, or known, or heard by such a mind, for it has gained all-knowledge, and for that reason it is called 'illuminating.' "

(16) The Buddha said: "Those who have passions are never able to perceive the Way; for it is like stirring up clear water with hands; people may come there wishing to find a reflection of their faces, which, however, they will never see. A mind troubled and vexed with the passions is impure, and on that account it never sees the Way. O monks, do away with passions. When the dirt of passion is removed the Way will manifest itself."

---

[1]The comparison here, of course, is obvious. Matthew 5:5. "Blessed are the meek: for they shall obtain mercy."

[2]The "dirt" of the mind is encompassed by the five "obscurities", which are envy, passion, sloth, vacillation, and unbelief.

(17) The Buddha said: "Seeing the Way is like going into a dark room with a torch; the darkness instantly departs, while the light alone remains. When the Way is attained and the truth is seen, ignorance vanishes and enlightenment abides forever."

(18) The Buddha said: "My doctrine is to think the thought that is unthinkable, to practice the deed that is not-doing, to speak the speech that is inexpressible, and to be trained in the discipline that is beyond discipline. Those who understand this are near, those who are confused are far. The Way is beyond words and expressions, is bound by nothing earthly. Lose sight of it to an inch, or miss it for a moment, and we are away from it forevermore."

(19) The Buddha said: "Look up to heaven and down on earth, and they will remind you of their impermanency. Look about the world, and it wil remind you of its impermanency. But when you gain spiritual enlightenment, you shall then find wisdom. The knowledge thus attained leads you anon to the Way."

(20) The Buddha said: "You should think of the four elements[1] of which the body is compsed. Each of them has its own name, and there is no such thing there known as ego. As there is really no ego, it is like unto a mirage."

(21) The Buddha said: "Moved by their selfish desires, people seek after fame and glory. But when they have acquired it, they are already stricken in years. If you hanker after worldly fame and practice not the Way, your labors are wrongfully applied and your energy is wasted. It is like unto burning an incense stick. However much its pleasing odor be admired, the fire that consumes is steadily burning up the stick."

(22) The Buddha said: "People cleave to their worldly possessions and selfish passions so blindly as to sacrifice their own lives for them. They are like a child who tries to eat a little honey smeared on the edge of a knife. The amount is

[1]Earth, water, fire, and air.

by no means sufficient to appease his appetite, but he runs the risk of wounding his tongue."

(23) The Buddha said: "Men are tied up to their families and possessions more helplessly than in a prison. There is an occasion for the prisoner to be released, but householders entertain no desire to be relieved from the ties of family. When a man's passion is aroused nothing prevents him from ruining himself. Even into the maws of a tiger will he jump. Those who are thus drowned in the filth of passion are called the ignorant. Those who are able to overcome it are saintly Arhats."

(24) The Buddha said: "There is nothing like lust. Lust may be said to be the most powerful passion. Fortunately, we have but one thing which is more powerful. If the thirst for truth were weaker than passion, how many of us in the world would be able to follow the way of righteousness?"

(25) The Buddha said: "Men who are addicted to the passions are like the torch-carrier running against the wind; his hands are sure to be burned."

(26) The Lord of Heaven offered a beautiful fairy to the Buddha, desiring to tempt him to the evil path. But the Buddha said, "Be gone. What use have I for the leather bag filled with filth which you have brought to me?" Then, the god reverently bowed and asked the Buddha about the essence of the Way, in which having been instructed by the Buddha, it is said, he attained the Srotaapanna-fruit.

(27) The Buddha said: "Those who are following the Way should behave like a piece of timber which is drifting along a stream. If the log is neither held by the banks, nor seized by men, nor obstructed by the gods, nor kept in the whirlpool, nor itself goes to decary, I assure you that this log will finally reach the ocean. If monks walking on the Way are neither tempted by the passions, nor led astray by some evil influences, but steadily pursue their course for Nirvana, I assure you that these monks will finally attain enlightnement."

(28) The Buddha said: "Rely not upon your own will.

Your own will is not trustworthy. Guard yourselves against sensualism, for it surely leads to the path of evil. Your own will becomes trustworthy only when you have attained Arhatship."

(29) The Buddha said: "O monks, you should not see women. [If you should have to see them], refrain from talking to them. [If you should have to talk], you should reflect in a right spirit: 'I am now a homeless mendicant. In the world of sin, I must behave myself like unto the lotus flower whose purity is not defiled by the mud. Old ones I will treat as my mother; elderly ones as elder sisters; younger ones as youngers sisters; and little ones as daughters.' And in all this you should harbor no evil thoughts, but think of salvation."

(30) The Buddha said: "Those who walk in the Way should avoid sensualism as those who carry hay would avoid coming near the fire."

(31) The Buddha said: "There was once a man who, being in depair over his inability to control his passions, wished to mutilate himself. The Buddha said to him: 'Better destroy your own evil thoughts than do harm to your own person. The mind is lord. When the lord himself is calmed the servants will of themselves be yielding. If your mind is not cleansed of evil passions, what avails it to mutilate yourself?' " Thereupon, the Buddha recited the gatha,

"Passions grow from the will,
The will grows from thought and imagination:
When both are calmed,
There is neither sensualism nor transmigration."

The Buddha said, this gatha was taught before by Kashyapabuddha.

(32) The Buddha said: "From the passions arise worry, and from worry arises fear. Away with the passions, and no fear, no worry."

(33) The Buddha said: "Those who follow the Way are like unto warriors who fight single-handed with a multitude of foes. They may all go out of the fort in full armor; but among them are some who are faint-hearted, and some who

go halfway and beat a retreat, and some who are killed in the affray, and some who come home victorious. O monks, if you desire to attain enlightenment, you should steadily walk in your Way, with a resolute heart, with courage, and should be fearless in whatever environment you may happen to be, and destroy every evil influence that you may come across; for thus you shall reach the goal."

(34) One night a monk was reciting a sutra bequeathed by Kashapabuddha. His tone was so mournful, and his voice so fainting, as if he were going out of existence. The Buddha asked the monk, "What was your occupation before you became a homeless monk?" Said the monk, "I was very fond of playing the guitar." The Buddha said, "How did you find it when the strings were too loose?" Said the monk, "No sound is possible." "How when the strings were too tight?" "They crack." "How when they were neither too tight nor too loose?" "Every note sounds in its proper tone." The Buddha then said to the monk, "Religious discipline is also like unto playing the guitar. When the mind is properly adjusted and quietly applied, the Way is attainable; but when you are too fervently bent on it, your body grows tired; and when your body is tired, your spirit becomes weary; when your spirit is weary, your discipline will relax; and with the relaxation of discipline there follows many an evil. Therefore, be calm and pure, and the Way will be gained."

(35) The Buddha said: "When a man makes utensils out of a metal which has been thoroughly cleansed of dross, the utensils will be excellent. You monks, who wish to follow the Way, make your own hearts clean from the dirt of evil passion, and your conduct will be unimpeachable."

(36) The Buddha said: "Even if one escapes from the evil creations, it is one's rare fortune to be born as a human being. Even if one be born as human, it is one's rare fortune to be born as a man and not a woman.[1] Even if one be born

---

[1]Compare the Christian belief in I Corinthians 11:7. "For a man. . . . is the image and glory of God: but the woman is the glory of the man."

a man, it is one's rare fortune to be perfect in all the six senses. Even if he be perfect in all the six senses, it is his rare fortune to be born in the middle kingdom. Even if he be born in the middle kingdom, it is his rare fortune to be born in the time of a Buddha. Even if he be born in the time of a Buddha, it is his rare fortune to see the enlightened. Even if he be able to see the enlightened, it is his rare fortune to have his heart awakened in faith. Even if he have faith, it is his rare fortune to awaken the heart of intelligence. Even if he awakens the heart of intelligence, it is his rare fortune to realize a spiritual state which is above discipline and attainment."

(37) The Buddha said: "O children of Buddha! You are away from me ever so many thousand miles, but if you remember and think of my precepts, you shall surely gain the fruit of enlightenment. You may, standing by my side, see me alway, but if you observe not my precepts, you shall never gain enlightenment."

(38) The Buddha asked a monk, "How do you measure the length of a man's life?" The monk answered, "By days." The Buddha said, "You do not understand the Way."

The Buddha asked another monk, "How do you measure the length of a man's life?" The monk answered, "By the time that passes during a meal." The Buddha said, "You do not understand the way."

The Buddha asked a third monk, "How do you measure the length of a man's life?" The monk answered, "By the breath." The Buddha said, "Very well, you know the Way."

(39) The Buddha said, "Those who study the doctrine of the Buddhas will do well to believe and observe all that is taught by them. It is like unto honey; it is sweet within, it is sweet without, it is sweet throughout; so is the Buddhas' teaching."

(40) The Buddha said: "O monks, you must not walk on the Way as the ox that is attached to the wheel. His body moves, but his heart is not willing. But when your hearts are

in accord with the Way, there is no need of troubling yourselves about your outward demeanor."

(41) The Buddha said: "Those who practice the Way
might well follow the example of an ox that mrches through
the deep mire carrying a heavy load. He is tired, but his
steady gaze, looking forward, will never relax until he come
out of the mire, and it is only then that he takes a respite.
O monks, remember that passions and sins are more than
the filthy mire, and that you can escape misery only by
earnestly and steadily thinking of the Way."

(42) The Buddha said: "I consider the dignities of kings
and lords as a particle of dust that floats in the sunbeam. I
consider the treasure of precious metals and stones as bricks
and pebbles. I consider the gaudy dress of silks and brocades
as a worn-out rag. I consider this universe as small as the
holila (?) fruit. I consider the lake of Anavatapta as a drop
of oil with which one smears the feet. I consider the various
methods of salvation taught by the Buddhas as a treasure
created by the imagination. I consider the transcendental
doctrine of Buddhism as precious metal or priceless fabric
seen in a dream. I consider the teaching of Buddhas as a
flower before my eyes. I consider the practice of Dhyâna as
a pillar supporting the Mount Sumeru. I consider Nirvana
as awakening from a day dream or nightmare. I consider the
struggle between heterodox and orthodox as the antics of
the six [mythical] dragons. I consider the doctrine of sameness as the absolute ground of reality. I consider all the
religious works done for universal salvation as like the plants
in the four seasons."

The Surangama Sutra
Selections from Books I and II

Ananda, on his return, beholding Buddha, bent himself to the ground in adoration, and shed a flood of (grateful) tears; at the same time, he was filled with regrets which had afflicted him from the first, that he yet remained among the number of the inferior disciples of his Master,[1] not having arrived at any advanced possession of sacred wisdom, although he had ever been most diligent (in his efforts) and in his earnest inquiries of the several Tathagatas, as to the means of perfecting himself in wisdom—that is to say, the perfect attainment of Samadhi, of complete efficacy (Samajna), the most excellent means of deliverance. And now again on this occasion there were before him countless Bodhisattvas[2] and the great Rahats of the ten regions, and Pratyeka Buddhas, all anxiously expecting to hear the joyful tidings, awaiting silently the enunciation of the sacred intentions of the mode of instruction about to be adopted.

Then Buddha addressed Ananda: "You and I, Ananda, are of one blood, related by the consanguinity of our parents; tell me, then, what it was first stirred your heart in my religious system—what excellences did you see of such per-

---

[1]Ananda is generally spoken of as the first of the "To-wan," *i.e.*, inferior disciples (Sekha). The Chinese expression is doubtless identical with that found in the Sanscrit and Pali.
[2]Bodhisattvas were believed by Mahayana Buddhists to be incarnations of Buddha—returned to earth in order to help enlighten and convert mankind. A loose Western parallel for arhat is "saint."

suasive character as to induce you to forsake and quit the fascinations of the world?"

Ananda replied thus to Buddha: "Seeing in Tathagata the thirty-two superior marks,[1] of such superlative beauty, your person bright and ruddy as crystal, and ever reflecting in myself that these marks were not those which the lusts of the flesh produce—for it is plain that the nature of the passions being turbulent and polluting, the humors of the body would in consequence be rank, and the pus secreted by the blood also turgid and irregular, preventing anything like the production of such excellences as mark the person of Tathagata, shining like gold in their collected splendor—beholding these signs in your person, therefore I followed Buddha with shaven crown."

'Buddha replied: "Well said, Ananda! but now (let me tell you something more), which you should be equally assured of, viz., that the whole world of sentient creatures, from the first till now, have been involved in the nexus of (endless) births and deaths, from the fact of their ignorance of the 'ever fixed and true state of Being (heart), essentially pure, and substantially glorious'; and so, by adopting every kind of idle speculation without any truth, men have been involved in the net of incessant renewals of existence. As you therefore now desire to investigate (the character of) that wisdom which admits of no further advance, with a view to eliminate (in yourself) the glorious powers of your original nature, you must first of all consent with a true heart to reply to my questions. The Tathagatas of the ten regions agreeing in observing this one method, have thus escaped from the maze of life and death, all of them possessing an upright heart; the words which they employed were therefore true.

---

[1]That is, the thirty-two maha-purusha-lakshana, or thirty-two marks of a great man. It should also be noted that the Chinese word for the Buddha, meaning "such-come" as translated by Lin Yutang, serves the dual purpose of characterizing both the Buddha and perfect wisdom of the godhead (Tathagataship), which is attainable by any man. There is no personal or anthropomorphic "God" in Buddhism and any man can achieve enlightenment and Buddhahood.

Thus, from first to last founding their conduct on this principle, throughout the whole of their previous career they ever avoided the danger of grievous error. Ananda, I now interrogate you!—when first you were conscious of a feeling of preference for the thirty-two superior marks of Tathagata, using what means of sight (did you arrive at this state?) and who was it that felt the pleasure of preference for me?"

Ananda replied: "World honored one! In this way I arrived at this pleasurable preference, by using my mind and my sight. My eyes gazing on you beheld the superlative excellences of Tathagata, and my mind was sensible of the birth of the delight of love; it was thus this condition was produced that made me desire to come out of the tangled influences that bound me to life and death."

Buddha replied to Ananda: "According to your words just uttered, the true ground of your pleasurable affection is to be sought in the mind and the eye. But if you know not the precise location of these powers, then you can never get rid of the dust-troubles that affect your conduct—just as though a king od a district, on account of the ravages of a band of robbers, were to equip a military force to expel them, the first requisite would be that the soldiers should know where aout the robbers were secreted. So as it is on account of the false judgments of your mind and sight that you are detained in the stream of perpetual transmigrations, I dreamed o you —say! where is the local habitat of this mind and of this sight of which you speak?"

Ananda, replying to Buddha, said: "World honored one! all the ten different kinds of being which exist in the world agree in considering that the intelligent mind resides within the body; whilst it is evident to every one beholding the blue lotus-shaped eyes of Tathagata, that *they* are in the face of Buddha; from which I conclude on this occasion that the four organs of sense[1] and the four objects of sense, combin-

[1]That is, sight, hearing, smelling, tasting. It means, of course, that these senses or organs of sense reside in the face; the other two senses, viz., touch and operation of mind, reside elsewhere.

ing their several offices here in my face—that the seeing eye is without me in my head, and the understanding heart within me in my body."

Buddha replied to Ananda thus: "Ananda, at this moment you are seated in the preaching-hall of Tathagata, look out now and see the trees of the Jetavana, and tell me where are they situated?"

"World honored one! this great storied religious preaching-hall is situated in the garden of Anathapindada (the friend of the orphans); and so the trees of the Jetavana must be of necessity outside the hall."

"Ananda, as you sit here in the hall, what is it (your eyes) first behold?

"World honored one, as I sit in the hall I first of all see Tathagata. Next I behold the great Assembly. Then looking outside, I see the varied trees of the garden."

"Ananda, as you behold the trees outside the hall, what is the medium through which you gaze on them?"

"World-honored one! the windows of this great preaching-hall being opened—therefore, as I sit here, I am able to obtain the extensive view which meets my eye beyond the hall!"

At this time the world-honored one, located in the midst of the great congregation, slowly unbaring his golden-clored arm, placed his hand on the head of Ananda, and explained to him and the rest ofthe great assembly that there was a Samadhi called Ta-fuh-teng-shau-leng-yan-wang, which admits of the exercise of countless active virtues, by means of which the Tathagatas of the ten regions as it were through this as a sole means of salvation having emerged, have quickly arrived at the state of infinite perfection. "Do you therefore attentively listen whilst I explain the character of this condition." Ananda, bowing down to the ground, humbly accepted the merciful intimation.

Buddha then addressed Ananda: "According to your statement, whilst your body is located in the preaching hall, the windows being open, you are enabled to gaze at the garden trees; tell me, then, if it is likewise possible for any person within this hall not to be able to see Tathagata and yet to behold the objects without the precincts?"

Ananda replied, saying: "World-honored one, it is clearly impossible to suppose that anyone withn the hall, not being able to see Tathagata, could yet behold the trees and the rivulets without the place."

"Ananda! apply the same reasoning to your assertion with respect to the mind. The spiritual character of your mind, bringing all things under its perception; if, according to your former statement, the groundwork of this perceptive faculty is within your body, then its first exercise would be to make itself acquainted with the inner parts ofthe body itself; so that all men should first be sensible of this priority of perception, embracing all that is within them, and afterwards extending to those things which are without. But how is it, then, in fact that we never meet with a man who is really able to see his own internal organs, e.gr., the heart, or liver, or kidneys, or stomach—or who can see the root-growth of his nails or hair—or who can trace the course of his nerves or the windings of his veins. I say, how is it at the time of the exercise of this power of perception (which you say resides within) a man cannot thus perceive what is within himself? or will it not follow on your own admission, that not being able to see that which is within, he cannot know what is without? You must admit, therefore, that this hypothesis regarding the seat of the knowing faculty, viz., that it is within the body, cannot be maintained."

Ananda, replying to Buddha, said: "World-honored one! I have also heard you discoursing with Manjusri and other eminent disciples, when you were engaged in the discussion of the question of the true (or sole) condition (of beng), say, that the intelligent mind was located neither within nor without.

"As far as I can understand the question, it seems that

we cannot say that the mind is placed within us, or else there is the difficulty of not seeing that which is within; and we cannot say that it is situated without us, or elser there is the difficulty about the relationship of mind and body, so that we are driven to the conclusion that there is a medium somewhere, so that the mind is neither within the body nor beyond it, *but between the two.*"

"You speak of 'between the two,' " said Buddha; "take care that this phrase does not deceive you, so that your 'between the two' means 'nowhere'. Let us investigate it. Where is the place of his middle point? Does it reside in the sense which perceives or in the thing perceived? if in the sense, then it resides necessarily in the body, and therefore it cannot be spoken of as a 'middle point.' But if this point be placed in the object perceived, then, as every such object is different, there must either be an index by which its presence can be determined or not; if not, then to all intents and purposes the place of its existence is as if it were no place; if there be an index to its existence, then this shows the changing character of this point, just as a man fixing a gnomon of a dial, having ascertained the exact middle point (or mid-day point), then looking due east, he fixes the west point, and looking due south he fixes the north point; thus the gnomon is no index to one fixed bearing, but to any bearing that is desired. So, then, if the intelligent mind be considered as residing in the middle of the object perceived, there can be no certain guide for ascertaining its particular position, but we may arrive at any conclusion, according to the caprice of each individual."[1]

Ananda said: "When I spoke of the middle point, I did not allude to these two kinds of explnation; but to this, that as Tathagata says that when the eye-sense unites with the object of sense, then eye-knowledge results; but as no knowl-

[1]The argument appears to be this: that the mind may reside in the midst of *any* object perceived, and that therefore it is impossible to fix its locality.

edge can reside in the mere object—but the eye has the power of distinguishing one object from another—so I say that the intelligent mind resides in the midst of that eye-knowledge which results from the exercise of this function of sight (or other sense)."

Buddha said: "If your intelligent mind resides in the middle of the sense and the object of sense, then the substance of this mind is either united with the two, or separated and distinct from the two.

"If united with the two, then there is a confusion of substance, so that the mind can no longer be regarded as a substantial unit; but there will be a mutual opposition betwixt the two hypostases, preventing the possibility of the middle entity of which you speak.

"But if there be no such union, then this intelligent mind must partly partake of the character of the sense which you say has the power of knowing, and party of the object of sense which you say has no such power. The mind, therefore, has no distinct character (nature); and if so, by what mark may you recognize it as it exists in the middle of these two opposing powers? You may conclude, therefore, that this hypothesis is not capable of proof."

Ananda addressed Buddha, saying: "World honored! formerly I saw Buddha in the society of Maudgalyayana, Subhuti, Pourna, Sariputra, four great Bodhisattva–Mahasattvas, discoursing on the law; on this occasion I heard the following assertion, frequently repeated, that the nature of the intelligent and discriminating mind was such, that it could not be said to be within the body, nor without it, nor in the middle point, but that that was rightly named the mind which in its very nature was without a local habitation, and without preference or active purpose. I should be glad to know, therefore, whether I may not define the intelligent mind as that which is 'indefinite,' and 'without partiality.' "

Buddha replied to Ananda: "You now say that the nature of this intelligent and discriminating mind is altogether intangible and indefinite; now let me ask, when you speak of space, of water, of land, of flying, of walking, and all the different conditions of existence, which are generally classified under the phrase, 'all forms of being,' you perhaps regard all these things with indifference and your mind is unattached to them—but do they exist or not?

"If they have no definite existence, then they are like the hair of the tortoise or the horn of the hare (mere fantasies); how then can youspeak of being indifferent to that which does not exist; for if there is such a thing as indifference, or such a state of being 'unattached,' then there must exist a real object from which you detach yourself, and therefore it cannot be spoken of as a 'nothing.' For that is 'nothing' which has no 'conditions' or 'qualities'; and where this absence of conditions does not exist, there cannot be an absence of that which is thus "conditioned.' So long, then, as you speak of the mind being 'unattached,' so long you presuppose the true existence of something which is unattached, where then, I again ask, is this something? Your theory, therefore, will not bear examination."

At this time Ananda, as he remained in the midst of the great congregation, rose from his seat, bared his right shoulder, bent down upon his right knee, and with closed palms, addressing Buddha, said: "I am indeed the very least of all Buddha's followers, ever grateful for the compassionate love which has brought me into this condition, and although I have left my home, am yet as a child dependent on a nurse, only a hearer and not arrived at any degree of perfection, unable even to destroy the evil influences of the sorceries of the Savara (Savakara, women), and therefore subjected by their enchantments to be led into the abodes of infamy; and all this from not knowing the precise limits of the Truth which Buddha declares. Oh! would that the world-honored one, of his great compassion, would open out to me the way of Samadhi, so as to enable me, when engaged in contemplation, to destroy all blinding influences."

Having spoke thus, Ananda prostrated himself on the earth, and all the congregation falling down, remained bent to the earth, anxiously awaiting the signal to arise and stand, as it would indicate the august purpose of Buddha to enter on the desired course of instruction.

At this time the world-honored one, from between his eyes (gates of the face), dispersed a succession of rays of light, brilliant and glorious as a hundred thousand suns. All the various worlds of Buddhas shook six times as with an earthquake, whilst the infinite lands of the ten regions of space in a moment appeared, whilst the mysterious spiritual power of Buddha caused all these worlds to unite as it were in one, and in the midst of this one world the entire body of Bodhisattvas, all coming to this common center, with closed hands, attentively listened.

Buddha then spake to Ananda: "The whole body of sentient creatures, from the first till now, has been (subject to) every kind of false impressions (inverted opinions); the consequence has been a spontaneous propagation of error, like the branches of the Gatcha tree;[1] so that men who have entered on the religious life have failed to attain to Supreme Wisdom, and have only arrived at the vain distinctions of Sravakas and Pratyeka Buddhas, or to the more imperfect forms of heretical belief. So it is that all the Devas Mara and their followers have come to this state from simple ignorance of the two original root-seeds f error, pursuing a confused form of religious discipline, attempting, as it were, to make serviceable bread out of hot sand, and from the false opinion that it was possible to do so, remaining for ever without food.

"Say, then, what are these two seeds of error? Ananda, the first is that which results from (ignorance about) the ever present root of lfe and death, which causes you and all beings to look on your conditioned mind as your true nature (or as possessing an independent nature). The second is (ignorance about) the true basis of the pure form of Nirvana, which generates in you that subtle form of inward knowledge which gives you the power of originating the influences that, in the end, lead you away from a sense of this subtle

[1]In Chinese *ngo-ch'a;* probably the banyan tree (ganjasana).

essence, so that though to your last day you live and act by
it, yet you know it not, and pass away into the different
forms of perishable being to which the power of error subjects you.

"Ananda, you now desire to know the way of Samadhi,
with a view to emerge from the sea of life and death. I ask
you, terefore"—meantime, Tathagata, stretching out his
golden-colored arm, bent together his five fingers, and said:
"Do you see me doing this, Ananda?"

"Yes, indeed, "Ananda replied; "I see you."

"What do you see," said Buddha?

"I see," Ananda replied, "Tathagata raising his arm,
bending his fingers into the form of a shining fist, dazzling
alike my mind and eye."

Buddha said: "Now, what is the instrument by which you
see all this?"

Ananada said: "I and all here present see this by the use
of your eyes."

Buddha addressed Ananda: "Answer me tuthfully! You
say that as Tathagata thus doubles his fingers together and
makes a shining fist of them, that your mind and eyes are
dazzled by the brilliancy of the same; but if it is your eyes
which see the fist, of what good (or account) is the mind
(heart) which you say my fist dazzles?"

Ananda replied: "Tathagata seems now to inquire as to
the particular locality in which this mind of which I speak
resides; and yet it is by means of this mind that I, of whom
you inquire, am able to investigate the question on which we
are speaking. I take it, therefore, that this mind is the power
by which I investigate."

Buddha replied: "No, no, Ananda, this is not your mind."

Ananda, in an agitated manner, quickly leaving his seat,
with raised hands stood upright before Buddha and said: "If
this is not my mind,[1] tell me what is its name?"

---

[1]The original word throughout this section might be translated "heart";
but this word is so ambiguous, I take it that the word corresponds to the
Sanscrit "atman" (self). Constant confusion develops in Chinese over the
word for heart, Hsin, which denotes also thinking and feeling.

Buddha answered: "This is but the perception of vain and false qualities, which, under the guise of your true nature, has from the first deceived you, and caused you to lose your original permanent (soul), and involved you in the nexus of the metempsychosis."

Ananda addressed Buddha again and said: "World-honored one! I am the favorite cousin of Buddha, and because my heart was moved with affection to your person, I left my home and became a disciple. My sole desire was to minister to Tathagata, and to the utmost bounds of the innumerable earths, to render service to all the Buddhas; my further hope was to arrive at supreme knowledge, making every effort to practice without exception the most arduous duties of my religious profession. All this was the inward purpose of my heart; and to this same source also I trace every disobedient act, and every evil thought against religion; but if these efforts and intentions do not result from the heart, then I take it I have no heart at all, and am just the same as the different kinds of inanimate earths and trees—for by removing this capability of knowledge, you do in fact make its existence impossible. Explain, then, I pray, this paradox of 'this not being my heart.' I deeply reverence and venerate your presence; and with all this great congregation am heartily desirous to have my doubts removed, by hearing that which we do not understand explained."

At this time the world-honored one began his explanation to Ananda and the rest of the congregation, desiring to excite in them a consciousness of that mind whih springs not from any earthly source. Sitting on his lion throne, therefore, he touched the top of Ananda's head and spoke thus: "Tathagata ever says, every phenomenon that presents itself to our knowledge is but the manifestation of Mind. The entire theory of the causes of production throughout the infinite worlds is simply the result of mind, which is the true substratum of all. Ananda, if all the varieties of "being" in the collection of worlds, down to the single shrub, and the leaf, or the fiber of the plant, tracing all these to their ultimate elements—if all these have a distinct and substantial nature of their own (as you say)—how much more ought the pure, excellent, and effulgent mind, which is the basis of all knowledge, to have attributed to it its own essential and substantial existence.

"If, then, you examine this question, and still prefer to call the discriminating and inquiring mind by the name of 'Heart,' you must at any rate distinguish it from the power that apprehends the various phenomena connected with the mere senses, and allow this a distinct nature. Thus, whilst you now hear me declaring the law, it is because of the sounds you hear there is a discriminating process within you; yet, after all sounds have disappeared, there still continues a process of thought within, in which the memory acts as a principal element, so that there is a mind acting as it were on the mere shadows of things.

"I do not forbid you to hold your own opinion on the question of this discriminative faculty, but I only ask you to search out the minutest elements of the question itself. If, after you have removed the immediate cause of sensation, there is still a discriminative power in the faculty of which we speak, then that is the true mind which you justly designate as yours; but if the discriminative power ceases to exist after the immediate cause which called it into exercise is removed, then this power is only a shadowy idea, dependent entirely on the presence of external phenomena; and therefore, when these are removed, the mind (as you regard it) becomes, as it were, a hair of the tortoise or the horn of the hare. So, then, the 'body of the law,' as it is called, would be the same as something which does not exist; and who then would strive after emancipation?"

At this Ananda and all the congregation sat silently lost in thought. Buddha then addressed Ananda thus: "Searchers after truth generally, although they may attain to the nine previous steps, seldom attain to the last deliverance found in the condition of a Rahat, and all this because they do not shake off the mistaken notion that this perishable and uncertain process of thought (which depends entirely on accidents) is true and real. And so it is that you, though you are one of the foremost of the Sravakas, have yet failed to attain to any degree of superior excellence."

※

Questions of King Prasenajit

At this time King Prasenajit, rising from his seat, addressed Buddha: "In former days, before I was brought to listen to the doctrinal teaching of all the Buddhas, I saw Katyayana Vairattiputra, who always said that this body of ours after death, was completely destroyed, and this he called Nirvana. And now, although I have met with Buddha, yet am not I altogether free from mistrusting doubts. Tell me, then, how I may obtain deliverance (from these doubts) and attain to the knowledge of this imperishable principle which you call the mind. We pray you in the name of this great assembly, many of whom are ignorant of this great truth, to enter on some further explanation of it."

Buddha said: "Maharajah! with respect to your present body, I would ask you, Is this body of yours like the diamond, unchangeable in its appearance, and ever fixed, and imperishable; or is it, on the other hand, changeable and perishable?"

The Rajah replied: "World-honored one! this body of mine, without doubt, in the end, after various changes, will perish."

Buddha said: "Maharajah! you have not yet experienced this destruction of the body; how, then, do you know anything about it?"

"World-honored one! replied the King, with respect to this transient, changeable, and perishable body; although I have not yet experienced the destruction of which I speak, yet I observe the case of things around me and ever reflect that all these things are changing—old things die, and new things succeed; there is nothing that changes not! thus the wood that now burns, will be soon converted into ashes; all things gradually exhaust themselves and die away; there is no cessation of this dying out and perishing. I may certainly know, then, that this body of mine will finally perish."

Buddha replied: "Just so!"

Maharajah: "Regarding yourself at your present age—now that you have begun to grow old—is your appearance the same as it was when you were a young child?"

"World-honored one! when in former years I was a young child—my skin was soft and delicate—gradually, as my years advanced, my pulses became stronger, and fuller, and now I am become an old man of sixty, my appearance has become withered and dried; my animal spirits low and sluggish; my hair white; my skin wrinkled—indicating that my future life will not be long. What, then, can be the comparison of my present appearance with that which I had when a child?"

Buddha said: "Maharajah! with respect to your appearance, was there ever a period when this change was not going on?

The Rajah answered: "World-honored one! this change is secret and mysterious, which I can never hope to explain. Just as winter gave way to summer, and we gradually have come to the present time, so is it with me. For the case is just this—when I was twenty years old, although I was still called by my juvenile appellative, yet my appearance had already become old compared with my first ten years; when I was thirty, I was still changed from what I had been at twenty years; and now, when I am sixty years and two, looking back at the time when I was fifty, I was then, compared with my present state, hale and strong. World-honored one! I find myself unconsciously changing; and, although I have instanced this gradual approach to death, by the changes I have experienced each decade of my life, yet if you will have me use more minute divisions, this change has been a yearly one; nay, each month and each day, the same decay has been going on; and, if I consider the case still more closely, every minute, every second (jana) there has been no fixity or continuance in one stay: I fully recognie the truth, therefore, that in the end my body must perish!"

Buddha said: "Maharajah! you confess that from witnessing these ceaseless changes, you arrive at the convictin that your body must perish! Let me ask—when this time for your body to perish arrives, are you cognizant of anything connected with yourself that will not perish?

Prasenajit Rajah, with his hands clasped before Buddha, replied: "Indeed, I am cognizant of no such (imperishable thing)."

Buddha said: "I will now explain to you the character of that 'nature' which admits of neither birth nor death." Maharajah, when you were a little child, how old were you when you first saw the River Ganges?"

The Rajah replied: "When I was three years old, my tender mother led me by the hand to pay my devotions to Jiva Deva, by this stream (flowing here in our sight), then it was I knew that this was (an affluent of) the Ganges."

Buddha said: "Maharajah, taking up your own illustration respecting your gradual alteration of appearance, through every decade of years, etc., of your life. You say that at three years of age you saw this river; tell me then, when you were thirteen years old, what sort of appearance had this river then?"

The Rajah replied: "Just the same as it had when I was three years old; and now I am sixty-two there is no alteration in its appearance."

Buddha said: "You now are become decrepit, white-haired, and wrinkled in face, and so your face has grown during successive years. Tell me, then, has the sight which enabled you to see the Ganges in former years become also wrinkled and increasingly so with your years?"

The King answered: "No! World-honored one."

Buddha said: "Maharajah! although, then, your face has become wrinkled, yet your power of sight has in its nature altered not. But that which becomes old and decrepit is in its nature changeable, and that which does not become so is unchangeable. That which changes again is capable of destruction, but that which changes not must be from its origin incapable of birth or death. How is it, then, that together with this imperishable power of sight you possess, there has crept in that which is of its nature perishable and changing? and how is it still more that those heretics, Makhali and others, say that after the death of the body there shall be a clean end of all life?"

The King hearing this, began to believe that after death there might perhaps be further life; and, therefore, with all the assembly accepted joyfully such a doctrine, and looked for further instruction.

Questions by Ananda

Then Ananda, rising from his seat, with clasped hands and prostrate form, addressed Buddha thus: "World-honored one! if this faculty of sight and hearing is of itself imperishable and incapable of birth or death, what then does your doctrine mean that I and others have lost our true nature, and all our actions are, as it were, inverted from their right purpose? Would that with your great compassion you would free me from the pollution of these doubts."

Immediately, Tathagata stretching forth his golden-colored arm, pointed down his beautiful fingers to the ground, and spoke thus: "Ananda, as you behold my Mudra hand, let me ask you, is it pointing up or down?"

Ananda replied: "World-honored, men generally regard the position which your hand now assumes, as downward; but, as for me, I know not what to call it—whether up or down."

Buddha addressed Ananda: "If, then, men generally call this positin downward, what would they call 'upward'?

Ananda replied: "Tathagata has but to raise his arm, and let his soft and silken hand point above into space, and that will be what men call 'upwards.' "

Buddha immediately lifted up his arm, and addressed Ananda, saying, "If this is what men call turning upside down—or head to tail—then understand this, that your body, compared with the mysterious body of Buddha, may be likewise illustrated by this similitude—for the body of Tathagata may be spoken of as upright in respect of its nature—but yours as of an inverted or misdirected nature.[1]

"Now, then, consider, I pray you, your body and Buddha's body—which you speak of as so related. These names signify something, but where is the location of these two things thus related to one another?"

At this time Ananda, with all the great congregation, looked at Buddha in blank perplexity—not knowing where these two bodies locally resided.

Buddha then, exercising his compassionate love—for the purpose of instructing Ananda and the great assembly—raised his voice, and thus addressed the whole assembly: "Illustrious disciples, my constant words are these—all the thousand connections of mind and body (matter), and the offspring of mind, to wit, the various modifications of ideas, all these are but what the heart originates; your mind and your body themselves are but things made manifest in the midst of this mysteriously glorious and true essence called the perfect heart. What, then, can be the meaning of losing this perfect heart, and this mysterious nature—is there not some deception in these words? (or, are they not owing to the deceptive influences which exist in the midst of the heart?)

"Dark and obscure is the space around us! In the midst of this sombre, gloomy space, by the capricious intertwinings of the darkness, forms are evoked. These capricious forms generate false reflections (in the heart), and from these spring the ideas of body. So the thousand connections which are aroused within the mind, purusing still further the vanishing and capricious forms without, there arises an end-

---

[1]The aim of this argument is to prove that the difference between the pure nature of Buddha and nature of man is one of relation only, as "upright" and "perverted" are different relations of the same thing.

less confusion—and so those ideas about the nature of the-mind are caused, which is the first great deception; it is concluded as a certainty that all these thoughts are fixed within the material body, in ignorance that this body, and all external phenomena, rivers, mountains, space itself, and earth, are but things which exist in the midst of this ever true and mysterious heart—just as if one should overlook the existence of the vast and innumerable oceans which are scattered through the universe, and center one's thoughts and investigations on a single bubble (or drop), regarding it as the true sea, and overlooking the countless real oceans. So is it when a man centers his thoughts on this deceitful idea, that his individual mind is the true basis of all which exists, and so is led to multiply such existences indefinitely. This is the inversion which I wished to explain by raising my arm after holding it downwards."

Buddha addressed Ananda as follows: "I ask you, now, at the present moment, although you have not attained complete emancipation (or complete spiritual power), yet exercising the spiritual power you possess, you are able to obtain a sight of the first Dhyani Heavens, without hindrance. Aniruddha, on the other hand, is able to see the whole of Jambudwipa as an Amra fruit (mango) in his hand; whilst the various Bodhisattvas are able to see the Great Chiliocosm; and the Tathagatas of the ten regions are able to see the infinite dust-like worlds (pure lands, Kshetras) scattered through space, compared with whose power of vision men can but see an inch before them.

"Ananda, supposing you and I are looking at the palaces occupied by the four kings;—on every side we see the sea and land, as we pass through space;—although we but dimly recognize, in the distant gloom, the various appearances of objects, yet there is nothing indistinguishable, so that you can clearly separate this from that. Now, I select a particular object for you to look at, and I ask you, What is this power of sight (personal substance),[1] and what is it makes these figures of objects which you see? Ananda, exert your utmost power of sight, let your observation reach to the palaces of the sun and moon, these external objects are not your personal substance; look at the seven golden mounts (that encircle the earth), observe well their whole circuit, although here you see everything clearly, still these external objects are not your personal substance; and now gradually behold the clouds, the birds, the moving winds and the clouds of dust, the trees and mounts and valleys, the herbs and shrubs, men and beasts, all these are not your personal substance.

"Ananda! the nature of all thse things which are scattered far and near around you is different, yet the power of sight which you possess, and by which you distinguish these several differences, remains the same. This power, excellent and bright, is clearly then your sight-nature.

"But if the seeing resides in the things, then you by your sight can see my sight; but if you say that we both see, or that our sight is the same, then, when the things which I see are removed from my sight, you ought to see the place of my not-seeing is applied unjustly to a place that can be seen; but if you cannot see the place where my not-seeing is, then there is a spontaneous annihilation of that which did exist, and why not an annihilation of you yourself.

"Once more, if you still suppose that your sight, when you have once beheld an object, is identified with that object, then that object ought to be able to see you, and thus

[1]Or, what or who is the real person that sees—and what is the character of the thing seen. Beal considers that "the whole of this translation is unsatisfactory." In a translation by Bhikshu Wai-tao and Dwight Goddard (*A Buddhist Bible*, Boston, Beacon Press, 1970, p. 139), this paragraph reads: "Let us consider the palaces of the conditions of water and earth and air. In those Heavenly Realms there may be seen similarities to light and darkness, and all other phenomena of this world, but that is because of the lingering memory of objects seen in this world. Under those Heavenly conditions. you would still have to continue making distinctions between yourself and objects. But, Ananda, I challenge you, by the perception of your sight, to detect which is my True Essence and which (simply) manifestation."

matter and spitie (nature) are blended; and so both you and I, and all material substances are one and the same; but this makes all argument impossible.

"Ananda! if, when you see me, this power of sight which you have is your own and not mine [and if, when I see you, my power of sight is mine and not yours], and yet this sight-nature is everywhere diffused, let me ask what *is* that which you speak of as 'not yours.' "

Ananda addressed Buddha and said: "World-honored one! if my sight be the same as the sight-nature of Tathagata, everywhere diffused, how is it that now, as I sit in this hall, I see but this alone? Is it possible that this power can be changeable, sometimes great and sometimes small? or can the impediment of a wall confine that which is so vast in its nature? I am unable to explain in what the just solution of this difficulty is found. Would that your compassionate love would exercise itself in explaining this matter on my account."

Buddha replied: "The mode of expression which refers all worldly things to some one of the descriptions, of great, small, within, without (square, round), and other modifications, results from the shifting nature of the phenomenal world, and in no way can it justly be attributed to the contraction or expansion of the seeing power.

"Just as though you had a square vessel—in this vessel you see a square hollow space—and I were to ask you, 'the square space that you see in this vessel, is it a permanent division of space or not?' if it is a fixed and distinct allotment, then substitute a round vessel for the square one, and the space ought not to be round; but if it is not a fixed shape, then, when you speak of the square space in a square vessel, there is a confusion of terms, for there is no such fixed thing as a square space. You say that you know not in what place to find the just solution of the question under consideration —the nature of all solutions like these is the same as the use of the conventional word 'space' of which I have been speaking—how, then, can you speak of seeking it in a particular place?

"Ananda, if you wish to arrive at a just apprehension of that which admits of no such limitation as round or square, then all you have to do is to dismiss the contraction of your idea to a square vessel, then the substantial character of space will be understood as that which admits of no such quality as round or square. How much rather, then, ought you to dismiss the idea of finding out the place where this quality of round space or square space dwells?

"So it is when you ask how it is that on entering this hall your sight becomes contracted, and on looking up to the sun it becomes extended, so that you can see the vast vault of heaven; and how, again, it is that the wall limits your view, but if a hole be made in it then your view is enlarged. I say so it is that this reasoning has no force.

"But all sentient creatures, from the very first, having been deceived by external objects, have lost their true nature, and have been carried by things here and there, and therefore have got hold of this idea of seeing much and seeing little.

"If, then, you are able to understand the real character of these external objects, then you become the same as Tathagata, your mind and body perfect, immoveably fixed, enabled to embrace in your grasp of mind the infinite worlds."

珞

Buddha addressed Manjusri and all the congregation: "The Tathagatas of the ten regions, and all the great Bodhisattvas, dwelling in their own self-contained state of Samadhi, to them sight and the associations of sight and all the attributes of thought are but as an empty flower of space (aurora), in their real character being unsubstantial; so then, sight and its associations being thus unreal when considered in connection with the excellent and glorious and pure state of True Knowledge (Bodhi), how can you refer to that condition the question of there being such things as seeing and not-seeing, or there not being such things.

"Manjusri! I now ask you, are you really Manjusri, or is there, in addition to this one, another Manjusri, or is this Manjusri whom I see before me the only Manjusri?"

"Just so! world-honored one! I am the true Masjusri, there is no other but me! for why? if there was another, then, as I am certain that I am myself, there cannot be room in the consciousness of this truth for any question of 'is there,' or 'is there not,' another."

Buddha said: "So do all the false appearances of the world (space), and this very excellent power of sight itself appear in the mind of the excellently bright and insurpassable glorious Bodhi; 'seeing' and 'not-seeing' are confused terms (*i.e.*, terms of no meaning in the supreme consciousness), and all the associations of seeing and hearing, just as the second moon which appears in the water; what is the moon? and again, what is the absence of this moon? Manjusri! there is but one moon, and (in its supposed consciousness) there can be no question of whether this one is itself, or whether there be another self.

"Wherefore, when you consider these various phenomenal appearances and the sight itself, you should consider them only as names which give rise to empty speculations; and from such elements you can never arrive at any firm conclusion of 'being' or 'not-being.' It is only from this true essence, which I call the 'glorious nature of mysterious wisdom,' that we can ever safely conclude as to any explanations of truth or falsehood."

Ananda addressed Buddha saying: "World-honored one! as I consider what you, our Supreme Lawgiver, say, that the associations (operations) of supreme wisdom are not confined to any spot; but that they are deep and ever fixed and self-contained, that the true nature is incapable of birth or death, it appears to me that this agrees generally with the discursive and inconclusive speculations of the old Brahma-

chari Savakara, and also inclines to the opinions of the
Nirgranthas and other heretics, who say 'that there is a true
personal *I* diffused throughout the whole universe.' I pray
you how does your opinion differ from theirs?

"World-honored one! Moreover, in the assembly at Lan-
kagiri, where, on the ground of your great compassion, you
also exhibited your doctrine;[1] those heretics there always
repeated their opinion about spontaneous phenomena, in
contradistinction to your theory of connected causes; but
now it seems to me that this nature of which you speak,
universally diffused, must exist spontaneously, as it neither
suffers life nor death; for the removal of all the unreal and
deceptive associations of sense, necessitates a contradiction
to the theory of connected causes, and makes us revert to
the 'spontaneous' theory of these heretics,—pray explain
this to me, lest I should fall into a false way of thinking, and
so that I may hold intact the truth of a real and essential
mind, and an excellent and ever-glorious nature."

Buddha said: "Ananda! notwithstanding the clear manner in which I have exhibited my doctrine, asking you
plainly and clearly for your opinions, I yet perceive that you
understand nothing, and so you are misled about this question of spontaneous existence. Ananda! if you must needs lay
hold of this opinion about self-caused or spontaneous existence, then the 'self' ought to be clearly discerned, the
substance and basis of this self-caused and self supporting
existence.

"Suppose, then, in the exercise of this mysterious and
excellently glorious vision, you are observing things around
you, tell me in what does the 'self' of this power consist—
is it due to the bright light of the sun? or is it attributable
to the presence of darkness? is it the existence of space
which constitutes the ground-work of this 'self?' or is it the
presence of obstacles that constitutes this self? Ananda! if

[1]This seems to refer to the subjects of discussion found in the Lan-
kavatara Sutra.

the bright presence of light is the groundwork, then, as this presence is the substantial basis of vision, what can be the meaning of seeing 'darkness.' If space is the basis of this 'self-caused' power, then, how can there be such a thing as an interruption of sight by any obstacle; or, if any of the various accidents of darkness be considered as the substantial basis of the 'self,' then, in the daylight the power of seeing light ought to disappear—what, then, is the meaning of the expression 'seeing light?''

Ananda said: "Of necessity I allow that this mysterious (bright) power of sight, its nature being opposed to that which is 'self-acting' or 'self-caused,' must depend on connected causes for its origin, but I would further inquire of Tathagata how the doctrine which he has enunciated today, can agree with this theory of connection of cause and effect."

Buddha said: "You now speak of 'cause and effect,' let me ask you—is the *cause* of your seeing (of which sight is the *effect*) in the light or darkness, or is it because of space, or of obstacles in space? Ananda! if this seeing nature depend for its existence (as an effect) on the light (as a cause), then, when it thus exists, it cannot be able to appreciate darkness (for then it would cease to be), and so on for the rest.

"You should be satisfied, therefore, that this subtle power of sight, essentially glorious, depends not for its existence, either on cause or connection, it is not what is termed self-caused, nor yet the opposite of this. In its origin it admits not of negation or the absence of negation; it agrees not with positive assertion or the absence of it; it is independent of all conditions and also of all phenomena (laws).

"Now then, perhaps, you will say how can we apprehend or lay hold of this heart (self) which exists in the midst of all these phenomena, especially in consideration of the infinite number of foolish theories which men have started about conditions of being and divisions of terms; you might as well, with the palm of the hand moving through space in a thousand fantastic ways, expect the space to lay hold of your hand (or to lay hold of space)."

Ananda addressed Buddha, saying: "World-honored one! if it is necessary to disconnect this sight-nature from all causes or concatenations, tell me what it is you mean by saying that the sight-nature is influenced by or dependent on four associations, viz., by space, light, mind, and the eye. What is this theory?"

Buddha said: "Ananda! this doctrine of mine concerning the conditional connections of things is not my highest flight of doctrine.

"Ananda! I again ask you—men say 'I am able to see.' What is this thing they call seeing? and what is 'not-seeing'?"

Ananda said: "Men, by means of sun or moon or lamplight, behold every kind of phenomenon; they say then 'I see'; in the absence of these they say 'I see not.' "

"Ananda! if, in the absence of these three kinds of light, there is no 'seeing,' then a man certainly ought not to see the dark; if he is obliged to see the darkness, this darkness being only the absence of light, how can you say he does *not* see in the dark? Ananda! if when a man cannot see the light you say he cannot see at all; and when he is in the light you say he cannot see the (what is called) darkness, then this term of 'not-seeing' is unfixed, it has two marks by which it may be known; if, then, these two conditions of 'not-seeing' should become mutually intermixed, then your sight-nature must disappear and become suddenly a nonentity. Know, therefore, that the word 'seeing' is rightly applied, whether it be dark or light. What, then, is the meaning of the expression 'not-seeing'?

"Therefore, Ananda! you ought to know that when you see the light, the seeing does not depend on the light; when you see the darkness, the seeing does not depend on the darkness; when you see space, the seeing is not concerned with the idea of space; and so also with the limitations of space.

"These four deductions being settled, then we proceed to say that when we exercise the power of sight through the medium of this very sight power, that, even then, seeing does not depend on this sight-power; nay, whilst 'seeing,' we may be still at a distance from 'true sight,'—nor by the exercise of sight do we necessarily exercise the power of 'true sight,'—how much less, then, can we speak of connected causes, or self-causation, or agreement of the object and subject, as constituting true sight.[1]

You Sravakas, having only a limited perception, cannot attain to (through the false mediums around you) the idea of a true and perfectly tranquil condition of being. I, therefore, now lead you, and on your part there should be a virtuous resolution to reflect narrowly on what I say, lest you should mistake the true way to Supreme Knowledge (Enlightenment)."

Ananda addressed Buddha, saying: "World-honored one! when Buddha for our sakes, who were but half-enlightened, exhibited the system of 'connected causes,' and the principle of 'self-causation,' and the conditions of 'agreement and non-agreement (of relations),' 'our minds could only partially receive the truth; and now, in addition to all this, we hear the doctrine 'that seeing is independent of sight.' Oh! would that your peculiar compassion for the ignorant would move

[1]Samuel Beal considers this argument difficult to translate. He writes that it seems to imply that "sensuous vision," "sight-power," and "sight-nature" are distinct questions. The three theories with which this part of the Sutra deals are that the exercise of sight depends on (1) the connection of cause and effect; (2) and that it is self-caused; and (3) that it is the result of harmonious combination. Dwight Goddard and Bhikshu Wai-tao translate this paragraph as: "Ananda, you should understand the significance of those four things, for when you are speaking of the perception of sight you are not referring to the phenomena of seeing with the eyes, but to the intrinsic perception of sight that transcends the experiential sight of the eyes, and is beyond its reach. Then how can you interpret this transcendental perception of sight as being dependent upon causes and conditions, or nature, or a synthesis of all of them? Ananda, are you of all the Arahats so limited in understanding that you cannot comprehend that this Perception of Sight is pure Reality itself?" (A Buddhist Bible, ibid., p. 149.).

you to bestow on us the eye of wisdom, and open out for us these difficulties, so that we might all obtain perfect understanding!" Having thus spoken, his tears falling in great abundance, he prostrated himself before Buddha awaiting the sacred will.

At this time the world-honored one, compassionating the case of Ananda and the great congregation, conceived the desire to exhibit for their benefit the great Dharani, the all-important mode of preparing the way to the Samadhis; he, therefore, spoke to Ananda, and said: "Although of such vigorous mind, you are as yet only a hearer, and your heart but little versed in the exceedingly mysterious and minute exercises of Samadhi—you should, therefore, attentively listen whilst I open out and distinguish for your sake the true road to this, and enable you and other imperfectly instructed disciples to obtain the fruit of Bodhi.

"Ananda! all sentient creatures are involved in the net of transmigration from two principal errors (inversions); these errors lead to false distinctions of sight, which give rise to birth, and generate the causes of the circle of repeated existencies. Say, then, what are the two views—first, all creatures having become entangled in different destinies, look at things through a mistaken medium; second, all creatures using the distinctions of sight, already adopted, are equally involved in these false apprehensions of things.

"Say, then, what description is this, 'of being entangled in different destinies (karmas),' and thus taking wrong views of things? Ananda! it is like a man whose eye is afflicted with a cataract: at night, when the light of the lamp shines before him, he thinks he sees a round shadow encircling the flame, composed of the five colours interlacing one another.

"What think you with regard to the perception of this round effulgence encircling the flame of the night lamp— is the beautiful color in the lamp, or is it in the eye? Ananda! if it is in the lamp, then why does not a man whose sight is healthy see it? if it is in the sight of the person, then, as it is the result of an act of vision, what name shall we give to the power that produces these colors?

"Again, in continuation, Ananda! if this circular halo has a distinct existence independent of the lamp, then, if it should happen that the person so described should approach the hanging screen and look at it, there ought to be the same circular halo on that also; but if this appearance has a distinct existence independent of sight, then it ought to appear without using the eyes, but then how can we say that it is a person with cataract who sees the halo?

"We conclude, therefore, that the object[1] looked at, i.e., the flame, is dependent on the lamp, that the circle is the result of imperfect vision, that all such vision is connected with disease, but that to see the cause of disease (the cataract) is curative of the disease itself.[2] So that, when the disease is once known, we cannot say justly that this lamp (circle) is (a disease of) sight; still less can we say that in the midst of all this there is neither lamp nor sight.

"So in the case of seeing a second moon in the water, we know that this partakes neither of the substance of the true moon, nor is there any circle of water. What then? the effort which completes the full apprehension of this second moon, in the case of those who have supreme wisdom, cannot be called an effort of their essential knowledge, which involves the question, 'Is this the true moon or not?' or, 'If I put my power of sight on one side, is there no such thing as seeing?' —so also, in the previous question about the cataract on the eye—causing the appearance of a halo round the lamp—it is no part of the wise man to inquire, 'Is this the lamp's fault, or the sight's fault?' Much less is it right to divide the question further into, 'What would be the consequence of

---

[1]The symbol "sih" has two meanings, either "color" or "matter."

[2]That is, when once the disease is known as a disease, then no ill effect can follow; as, for instance, if a person with diseased sight knows that the fanciful colors, etc., which he sees are merely the result of his imperfect organs of vision, then he is, so far, restored to perfect vision, or at any rate he is freed from self-delusion.

the lamp being taken away, or the sight being taken away?'[1]

"So, then, just what you and other creatures see now, viz., mountains, rivers, countries, and lands; all this, I say, is the result of an original fault of sight—mistaking sight for the association of sight—the cataract, as it were, on the true and ever-glorious power of sight which I possess.

"If, then, this imaginary power of sight be, as it were, a cataract on the eye of my true sight, then it follows, as a matter of course, that the pure and bright mind of my true science in seeing all these unreal associations is not afflicted with this imperfection: that which understands error is not itself in error; so that, having laid hold of this true idea of sight, there will be no further meaning in such expressions as hearing by the ears, or knowing by the sight.

"This faculty, then, which we, and all the twelve species of creatures possess, and which we call sight—this is the same as the cataract on the eye—it is the imperfection of true sight; but that true and original power of vision which has become thus perverted, and is in its nature without imperfection—that cannot properly be called, what we mean when we say, sight.

"If, then, we are only able to banish and destroy all these influences which have blended and intermixed with the true, so that they shall no longer so intermingle, then once more we may put an end to the causes of life and death, and arrive at the perfection of Bodhi—obtain the deathless nature, the 'ever pure and composed heart,' the true and unchangeable condition of accomplished wisdom.

"Ananda! although you have previously allowed and understood that the pure and ever-glorious state of Buddha's original being is in its nature totally disconnected from any causal concatenation, and also from any self-caused influences, yet your thoughts on the subject are still not entirely clear; you must, therefore, understand further that this nature is not dependent on harmony or union (with other

---

[1] I omit, from this point, sections that appear redundant.

things), and is not the result of any such supposed harmony or union.

"Ananda! I now again refer to the objects of sense which like dust surround us, and ask you, You still regard all these different illusory theories which exist in the world, touching harmony and union, causal concatenation, and so on, as having a real nature, and so you create doubts in yourself about the character of the State of Perfect Knowledge, as if this also were the result of harmony and union? I ask you, therefore, if it is so, with respect to the true and essential power of sight you possess, does this power depend on its harmony with the light, or its harmony with the darkness, or its harmony with that which is penetrable, or its harmony with that which is impenetrable?

"If you say that this excellent gift of sight is the result of a union either with light or darkness or space or matter —if with light, then in darkness how can there be such a thing as seeing the darkness; and so on for the rest."

Ananda addressed Buddha and said: "World-honored one! as I grasp the subject, I conceive that this excellent and original state of wisdom has no harmony with, or union with, the associations of sense or the confused thoughts of the mind."

Buddha said: "You say now again that this state of wisdom is not the result of harmony or union (with external associations). I ask you, therefore, with respect to this excellent power of sight which is not the result of such harmony or union, is the *negation* of which you speak attributable to the light, or the darkness, etc.;—if this negation is owing to an absence of harmony existing in the light, then there must be a distinct line of division between this light and the power of sight. Consider, then, where is the local habitation of the light, and where the habitation of your sight; if they both occupy one place, how can there be opposition betwixt them. Ananda! if the light occupies an independent space, then in that space there can be no seeing; for there can be no connection there between the sight and light, and therefore there can be no knowledge of the place where this light dwells; how, then, can there be any settled division between the two?

"Again, this excellent power of sight depending on no harmony or union, is it the negation of light-union, or darkness-union, etc.; if it is the negation of light-union, then light and sight, regarded as distinct natures, are at cross purposes and unfit for one another, like the ear and light, there can be no mutual fitness for connection; but if the sight cannot apprehend the distinct place of the light, then how can there be any distinct arrangement for the admission of light, say, on the part of the potter (who makes his vessels semi-lucid); and so on for the rest.

"Ananda! You still, perhaps, misunderstand the truth that all the vanishing appearances around us, and all the flitting, unreal conditions of being, of which we speak, have, nevertheless, a distinct place of origin, and also disappear according to a fixed order; for those so-called vanishing qualities are really part and parcel of the substance of the excellent Body of Wisdom—even down to the five skandhas, and the six ayatanas, and the twelve upasthanas, and the eighteen dhatus—all these, and the ideas of causal concatenation, etc.—all have a distinct origin, and because of the cessation of these causal influences they are said to disappear; but to ascertain the precise point when they come and when they go is not possible: we must look for that in the Supreme Nature of the First Cause, and beyond that we can ascertain nothing."

Selections From Book V

Ananda said: "Notwithstanding all the World-honored one has said, I am still at a loss to know what is the bondage under which you say we all live, and what is the deliverance of which you speak."

Then Buddha, touching the head of Ananda, forthwith the ten earths shook six times, and from each Buddha throughout the countless universe proceeded bright celestial rays, which all came and alighted on the head of Buddha in the garden of Jeta; and at the same time Ananda and all the congregation heard these words proceeding from the different mouths of all the Buddhas:

Well spoken, Ananda! you are now desirous to know the character of that ignorance which is the origin of the perpetual succession of birth and death; and, satisfied that your six senses have no power to free you from the dondage, you desire to find out the nature of the unsurpassable knowledge which alone can give you the freedom and rest which these six senses never can."

Still Ananda was unsatisfied, and asked for explanation.

Buddha said "Ananda! the sense and the objects of sense are one at root—bondage and freedom are not two. The nature of knowledge (or knowledge and nature) is empty and vain, just as a sky-flower.

"Ananda! from the objects of sense arises knowledge (of the possession of sense); from the senses themselves come qualities of objects: both qualities and sight (knowledge) are as the empty bubble.

"Wherefore we conclude that your method of establishing your knowledge by the exercise of the cognitions of sense, is false, and the same as the original irnorance; whereas the conviction that these cognitions bring you no reall knowledge—this is nirvana—pure truth without alloy."

At this time the World-honored one, wishing to give weight to the delivery of this system of truth, spoke the following gathas:—

"The Pure Nature, as to its substantial being, is empty; the influences, therefore, that produce birth are as a magical delusion. The absence of action, and the absence of beginning and end—these also are false ideas, like a sky-flower. The world "false" does but originate (manifest) that which is true—false and true are together equally false; and yet, again, the assertion that this or that is opposed to truth is itself opposed to truth. What, then, means this phrase of seeing and that which is seen; for in the so-called world what true nature or power is there? Are not all things around us but as a bubble?

"The ground-cause of bondage and deliverance is the same; sages and philosophers walk not on different paths. Consider, then, and embrace the nature of this middle method: emptiness and reality are both alike false; deception and enlightenment are both alike founded on ignorance. Once dream of enlightenment (*i.e.*, of making that which was ignorant wise), and you may forthwith bid adieu to all idea of release.

"Get rid of the idea of successive causes of thraldom; forget also the idea of unity found by extirpating the six senses; select only as a basis of all the perfect and all-pervading essence, and then, entering the stream, you shall perfect in yourself the Divine Intelligence.

"But concerning the knowledge of remote causes, or the knowledge of past conditions of birth, whether true or whether not true, for fear of deception, of these things I never speak.

"The self-existing mind taking hold of (or "cleaving to," upadana) its own mind, then that which is itself contrary to delusion, of itself creates illusive phenomena; but not taking hold of (it), there is an absence of (the idea of) that which is contrary to illusion; and if this idea be never produced, then what foundation can there be for illusive phenomena?

"This is, indeed, the "mysterious Lotus," the precious wisdom of Vajra Raja, the magic Samadhi, leaping over all ignorance in the snapping of a finger. This is the true Abid-harma—the Bhagavan of the ten worlds—the one gate of Nirvana."

On this, Ananda and all the great congregation, hearing the profoundly merciful exposition of Buddha Tathagata contained in the lines of these gathas, so clear in their meaning, so lucid in their words, receiving enlightenment from their delivery, rejoiced with great joy.

Then Ananda, with closed hands, etc., addressed Buddha thus: "Although I have heard this profoundly merciful exposition of truth, yet is my heart not altogether able to reach the meaning of the doctrine of the six loosenings, excluding the idea of one reality. Would that the World-honored one would, for our sake, explain the meaning of this doctrine!"

At this time, Tathagata, sitting on his lion throne, arranged his Nivasana Robe, and gathered up his Sanghati, and taking hold of the table near him, made of seven precious substances, stretching forth his hand upon it, he took hold of the embroidered silken handkerchief which the Deva Ki-pi-lo (Kapila?) had given him.

And then, in the sight of the great congregation, he tied in it a knot, and, showing it to Ananda, said," What call you this?"

Ananda and all replied," This is called a knot."

On this Buddha repeated the act, and tied a second knot above the first, and said, "What call you this?"

They replied again," This also is a knot"; and on this he repeated the act, and, one after another, tied six knots, showing each to the assembly and asking the same question, receiving in each case a similar reply.

Buddha addressed Ananda:" When I first tied the handkerchief, you said it was made into a knot; yet the handkerchief itself is one piece of silk. How, then, can you speak of a second and a third knot?

Ananda replied: "World-honored! this precious embroidered handkerchief, originally woven from silken threads into its present form, although in itself essentially one substance, yet, as I imagine, when tied up into a knot, may be spoken of as knotted, even if there were a hundred; how much more in the present case, when there are but six. On what ground, then, does Buddha demur to the name given to each succesive act on his part?"

Buddha addressed Ananda: "You know, with respect to this valuable silk, that in its original character it is one; but when I tied the six successive knots, you replied on each case that the silk was knotted. You should clearly understand the limits of this inquiry then, that substantially this silk is one, but circumstantially, on account of the knots, it is different. Now tell me what you think; each knot I tied, down to the sixth, you replied was a different knot. I now propose to take this sixth knot, as you call it, and now, completing it, I ask do I affect the first knot?" Ananda replied: "No, World-honored one! as long as you preserve the six knots you have tied, this last cannot in any way be called the first, or affect it in its form."

Buddha said: "Thus, then, the six knots are not the same; and searching out the cause of their difference, it results from the one article called a handkerchief, of which they are made; and if you confuse the order or the reality of each of the six, you can obtain no exact idea of the whole: so it is with your six organs of sense."

Buddha addressed Ananda: "You must still bear with the illustration derived from this subject of the knots; suppose now, for instance, you did not wish to have any knots at all, but delighted in the idea of unity, how would you proceed?"

Ananda said: "If you keep these knots tied, then there must of necessity arise the point, this knot is this, and not that; so that the question of this and that is produced. If, then, you want to get rid of this question, all you have to do is to tie no knots, and then, indeed, you will not even have to consider the question of unity, for if there is no succession of knots, there can be no first knot. Buddha said, So it is, I say, the doctrine of the six loosenings excludes the idea of unity.

"From the first, your mind and your nature, being in disorder and confusion, there has existed a false excitement of a knowledge derived, e.g., from eight, and this knowledge, wildly excited, has produced eneldess deceptions; at last, worn out and fatigued with excessive action, the sight has caused the origination of objects of sense, as the eye fatigued sees in space fanciful figures and sky-flowers. But really, in the depth of the true power of sight, there lies no ground or cause for this confusion; and so from this excess of action have sprung up, as qualities and characteristics of this false appearance, the ideas of worldly phenomena—mountains and rivers and the great earth, life and death and Nirvana —all are alike but perishing qualities of a condioned existence."

Ananda said: "This excessive action I take to correspond to these knots: tell me, then, how to get rid of it."

Then Tathagata, with his hand, taking the knotted handkerchief, smoothed out the left part of it, and said, "It is now untied, Ananda?"

To which he replied, "No."

Then the World-honored one, shaking out the other part, with his hand smoothed it to the right, and said, "Is it now untied, Ananda?"

To which he replied, "No."

The World-honored one then added, "I have smoothed the silken napkin out, on the right and left, and yet you say it is not untied: tell me, then, how is it to be unloosed?"

To which Ananda said, World-honored! you must take the knot at the heart of it, and then separate the parts, and you will untie it."

Buddha replied: "Good, good, Ananda! if you wish to untie the knots, you must begin at the Heart."

On Trust in the Heart

The Perfect Way is only difficult for those who pick and
    choose;
Do not like, do not dislike; all will then be clear.
Make a hairbreadth difference, and Heaven and Earth are
    set apart;
If you want the truth to stand clear before you, never be for
    or against.
The struggle between 'for' and 'against' is the mind's worst
    disease;
While the deep meaning is misunderstood, it is useless to
    meditate on Rest.
It[1] is blank and featureless as space; it has no 'too little' or
    'too much';
Only because we take and reject does it seem to us not to
    be so.
Do not chase after Entanglements as though they were real
    things,
Do not try to drive pain away by pretending that it is not
    real;
Pain, if you seek serenity in Oneness, will vanish of its own
    accord.
Stop all movement in order to get rest, and rest will itself
    be restless;
Linger over either extreme, and Oneness is for ever lost.
Those who cannot attain to Oneness in either case will fail:
To banish Reality is to sink deeper into the Real;
Allegiance to the Void implies denial of its voidness.

[1]The Buddha-nature.

The more you talk about It, the more you think about It,
   the further from It you go;
Stop talking, stop thinking, and there is nothing you will not
   understand.
Return to the Root and you will find the Meaning;
Pursue the Light, and you will lose its source,
Look inward, and in a flash you will conquer the Apparent
   and the Void.
For the whirligigs of Apparent and Void all come from
   mistaken views;
There is no need to seek Truth; only stop having views.
Do not accept either position,[1] examine it or pursue it;
At the least thought of 'Is' and 'Isn't' there is chaos and the
   Mind is lost.
Though the two exist because of the One, do not cling to
   the One;
Only when no thought arises are the Dharmas without
   blame.
No blame, no Dharmas; no arising, no thought.
The doer vanishes along with the deed,
The deed disappears when the doer is annihilated.
The deed has no function apart from the doer;
The doer has no function apart from the deed.
The ultimate Truth about both Extremes is that they are
   One Void.
In that One Void the two are not distinguished;
Each contains complete within itself the Ten Thousand
   Forms
Only if we boggle over fine and coarse are we tempted to
   take sides.
In its essence the Great Way is all-embracing;
It is as wrong to call it easy as to call it hard.
Partial views are irresolute and insecure,
Now at a gallop, now lagging in the rear.
Clinging to this or to that beyond measure

[1]Assertion and Negation.

The heart trusts to bypaths that lead it astray.
Let things take their own course; know that the Essence
Will neither go nor stay;
Let your nature blend with the Way and wander in it free
    from care.
Thoughts that are fettered turn from Truth,
Sink into the unwise habit of 'not liking'.
'Not liking' brings weariness of spirit; estrangements serve
    no purpose.
If you want to follow the doctrine of the One, do not rage
    against the World of the Senses.
Only by accepting the World of the Senses can you share
    in the True Perception.
Those who know most, do least; folly ties its own bonds.
In the Dharma there are no separate dharmas, only the
    foolish cleave
To their own preferences and attachments.
To use Thought to devise thoughts, what more misguided
    than this?
Ignorance creates Rest and Unrest; Wisdom neither loves
    nor hates.
All that belongs to the Two Extremes is inference falsely
    drawn—
A dream-phantom, a flower in the air. Why strive to grasp
    it in the hand?
'Is' and 'Isn't', gain and loss banish once for all:
If the eyes do not close in sleep there can be no evil dreams;
If the mind makes no distinctions all Dharmas become one.
Let the One with its mystery blot out all memory of com-
    plications.
Let the thought of the Dharmas as All-One bring you to the
    So-in-itself.
Thus their origin is forgotten and nothing is left to make us
    pit one against the other.
Regard motion as though it were stationary, and what
    becomes of motion?

Treat the stationary as though it moved, and that disposes
    of the stationary.
Both these having thus been disposed of, what becomes of
    the One?
At the ultimate point, beyond which you can go no further,
You get to where there are no rules, no standards,
To where thought can accept Impartiality,
To where effect of action ceases,
Doubt is washed away, belief has no obstacle.
Nothing is left over, nothing remembered;
Space is bright, but self-illumined; no power of mind is
    exerted.
Nor indeed could mere thought bring us to such a place.
Nor could sense or feeling comprehend it.
It is the Truly-so, the Transcendent Sphere, where there is
    neither He nor I.
For swift converse with this sphere use the concept 'Not
    Two';
In the 'Not Two' are no separate things, yet all things are
    included.
The wise throughout the Ten Quarters have had access to
    this Primal Truth;
For it is not a thing with extension in Time or Space;
A moment and an aeon for it are one.
Whether we see it or fail to see it, it is manifest always and
    everywhere.
The very small is as the very large when boundaries are
    forgotten;
The very large is as the very small when its outlines are not
    seen.
Being is an aspect of Non-being; Non-being is an aspect of
    Being.
In climes of thought where it is not so the mind does ill to
    dwell.
The One is none other than the All, the All none other than
    the One.

Take your stand on this, and the rest will follow of its own
    accord;
To trust in the Heart is the Not Two, the Not Two is to trust
    in the Heart.
I have spoken, but in vain; for what can words tell
Of things that have no yesterday, tomorrow or today?

From the
Conversations of Shen-hui

1

The Master Shen-tsu asked Shen-hui: "You say that our Original Nature has the characteristics of the Absolute. In that case it has no color, blue, yellow or the like, that the eye can see. How then can one perceive one's Original Nature?" Shen-hui answered, "Our Original Nature is void and still. If we have not experienced Enlightenment, erroneous ideas arise. But if we awaken to the erroneous nature of these ideas, both the Awakening and the wrong idea simultaneously vanish. That is what I mean by 'perceiving one's Original Nature'." Shen-tsu again asked: "Despite the light that comes from the Awakening, one is still on the plane of Birth and Destruction. Tell me by what method one can get clear of Birth and Destruction?" Shen-hui answered, "It is only because you put into play the ideas of Birth and Destruction that Birth and Destruction arise. Rid yourself of these ideas, and there will be no substance to which you can even distantly apply these names. When the light that comes from the Awakening is quenched, we pass automatically into Non-being, and there is no question of Birth or Destruction."

2.

"The passions (klesa)," said the disciple Wu-hsing, "are boundless and innumerable. Buddhas and Bodhisattvas pass through aeons of austerity before achieving success. How was it that the dragon's daughter was instantaneously converted and forthwith achieved Complete Enlightenment?"

"Conversion," said Shen-hui, can be either sudden or gradual; both delusion and the Awakening can come to pass slowly or swiftly. That delusion can go on for aeon after aeon and the Awakening can come in a single moment is an idea that is difficult to understand. I want first of all to illustrate the point by a comparison; I think it will help you to understand what I mean. A single bundle of thread is made up of innumberable separate strands; but if you join them together into a rope and put it on a plank, you can easily cut through all these threads with one stroke of a sharp knife. Many though the threads may be, they cannot resist that one blade. With those who are converted to the way of the Bodhisattvas, it is just the same. If they meet with a true Good Friend who by skillful means brings them to immediate perception of the Absolute, with Diamond Wisdom they cut through the passions that belong to all the stages of Bodhisattvahood. They suddenly understand and are awakened, and see for themselves that the True Nature of the dharmas is empty and still. Their intelligence is so sharpened and brightened that it can penetrate unimpeded. When this happens to them, all the myriad entanglements of Causation are cut away, and erroneous thoughts many as the sands of the Ganges in one moment suddenly cease. Limitless virtues are theirs, ready and complete. The Diamond Wisdom is at work, and failure now impossible."

3

"What is the Void?" asked the Master of the Law Ch'ung-yüan. "If you tell me that it exists, then you are surely implying that it is solid and resistant. If on the other hand you say it is something that does not exist, in that case why go to it for help?" "One talks of the Void," replied Shen-hui, "for the benefit of those who have not seen their own Buddha-natures. For those who have seen their Buddha-natures the Void does not exist. It is this view about the Void that I call 'going to it for help'."

4

"You must not take it amiss," said Shen-hui to the Master of the Law Ch-ung-yüan and some others, "if I tell you the following story. Nowadays such a lot of people are giving instruction in Dhyana that students are becoming completely bewildered. I am afraid that among these instructors there may well be some that are bent upon leading students of religion astray and destroying the True Law—such teachers being in fact Heretics in disguise, or even the Evil One Mara himself. That is the reason why I tell you this story. Well, it was in the period Chiu-shih (700 A.D.). The Empress Wu Hou summoned the monk Shen-hsiu[1] to serve in the Palace and when he was about to leave his monastery . . . his followers, both laymen and monks, asked him how they were to carry on their spiritual exercises in his absence, and where they were to turn for guidance. 'You will have to go to Shao-chou,' said Shen-hsiu. 'You will find there a great Good Friend[2] It was to him that the great Master Hung-jen handed on the succession. That is the place to go to for Buddha's Law. They have it all there. If there is anything that you cannot decide about for yourselves, go there and you will be astonished' That Master really does understand the true principles of Buddhism.' Accordingly in . . . the third year of Ching-lung (709) Shen-hsiu's disciple Kuang-chi (affecting to carry out this advice) went to Hui-neng's monastery at Shao-chou and after spending about ten days there he went at midnight to the Master's cell and stole the Mantle of Succession. Hui-neng screamed and his disciples Hui-yüan and Hsüan-wu hearing him scream went to see what was wrong. Just outside Hui-neng's cell they met Kuang-chi, who grapsed Hsüan-wu's hand and warned him not to make any noise (as the Master was asleep). However, the two disciples thought they had better go and see if

---

[1]Leader of the Northern School of Dhyana.
[2]Hui-neng, leader of the Southern School.

Hui-neng was all right. 'Someone has been in my cell,' said Hui-neng when they came to him. 'He grabbed at the Mantle and carried it off' Presently a number of monks and some laymen too, both southerners resident at the monastery and visitors from the north, came to Hui-neng's cell and questioned him about the intruder. 'Was he a monk or a laymen?' they asked. 'I could not see,' said Hui-neng. 'Someone certainly came in, but whether he was a monk or a layman I can't say.' They also asked whether the man was a northerner or a southerner. As a matter of fact Hui-neng knew who the man was; but he was afraid that, if he mentioned his name, his own disciples might do Kuang-chi some injury. That was why he answered as he did. 'This is not the first time,' Hui-neng went on. 'It was stolen three times from my master Hung-jen, and Hung-jen told me that it was also stolen once from his master Tao-hsin. . . . This mantle is destined to bring to a head the quarrel between the monks and laymen of the south and those of the north. They will never meet save with sword or cudgel in hand.' "

The Platform Sutra of the Sixth Patriarch
Selections from the Tun-Huang Manuscript*

The Master Hui-neng called, saying: "Good friends, en-lightenment *(bodhi)* and intuitive wisdom *(prajña)* are from the outset possessed by men of this world themselves. It is just because the mind if deluded that men cannot attain awakening to themselves. They must seek a good teacher to show them how to see into their own natures. Good friends, if you meet awakening, [Buddha]-wisdom will be achieved.

"Good friends, my teaching of the Dharma takes medita-tion *(ting)* and wisdom *(hui)* as its basis. Never under any circumstances say mistakenly that meditation and wisdom are different; they are a unity, not two things. Meditation itself is the substance of wisdom; wisdom itself is the func-tion of meditation. At the very moment when there is wis-dom, then meditation exists in wisdom; at the very moment when there is meditation, then wisdom exists in meditation. Good friends, this means that meditation and wisdom are alike. Students, be careful not to say that meditation gives rise to wisdom, or that wisdom gives rise to meditation, or that meditation and wisdom are different from each other. To hold this view implies that things have duality—if good is spoken while the mind is not good, meditation and wis-

*Reprinted from the translation of Philip B. Yampolsky, *The Platform Sutra of the Sixth Patriarch*, The text of the Tun-Huang Manuscript, with the kind permission of Columbia University Press, New York.

dom will not be alike. If mind and speech are both good, then the internal and the external are the same and meditation and wisdom are alike. The practice of self-awakening does not lie in verbal arguments. If you argue which comes first, meditation or wisdom, you are deluded people. You won't be able to settle the argument and instead will cling to objective things, and will never escape from the four states of phenomena.[1]

"The *samādhi* of oneness is straightforward mind at all times, walking, staying, sitting, and lying. The *Ching-ming ching* says: 'Straightforward mind is the place of practice; straightforward mind is the Pure Land.' Do not with a dishonest mind speak of the straightforwardness of the Dharma. If while speaking of the *samādhi* of oneness, you fail to practice straightforward mind, you will not be disciples of the Buddha. Only practicing straightforward mind, and in all things having no attachments whatsoever, is called the *samādhi* of oneness. The deluded man clings to the characteristics of things, adheres to the *samādhi* of oneness, [thinks] that straightforward mind is sitting without moving and casting aside delusions without letting things arise in the mind. This he considers to be the *samādhi* of oneness. This kind of practice is the same as insentiency and the cause of an obstruction to the Tao. Tao must be something that circulates freely; why should he impede it? If the mind does not abide in things the Tao circulates freely; if the mind abides in things, it becomes entangled. If sitting in meditation without moving is good, why did Vimalakīrti scold Sāriputra for sitting in meditation in the forest?

"Good friends, some people teach men to sit viewing the mind and viewing purity, not moving and not activating the mind, and to this they devote their efforts. Deluded people do not realize that this is wrong, cling to this doctrine, and

[1]Philip Yampolsky notes that this probably refers to birth, being, change, and death, but may also refer to "four of the eight forms of misconception, beliefs in some form of ego (self, being, soul, person), mentioned in the Diamond Sutra."

become confused. There are many such people. Those who instruct in this way are, from the outset, greatly mistaken.

"Good friends, how then are meditation and wisdom alike? They are like the lamp and the light it gives forth. If there is a lamp there is light; if there is no lamp there is no light. The lamp is the substance of light; the light is the function of the lamp. Thus, although they have two names, in substance they are not two. Meditation and wisdom are also like this.

"Good friends, in the Dharma there is no sudden or gradual, but among people some are keen and others dull. The deluded recommend the gradual method, the enlightened practice the sudden teaching. to understand the original mind of yourself is to see into your own original nature. Once enlightened, there is from the outset no distinction between these two methods; those who are not enlightened will for long kalpas be caught in the cycle of transmigration.

If you do not think, then your nature is empty; if you do think, then you yourself will change. If you think of evil things then you will change and enter hell; if you think of good things then you will change and enter heaven. [If you think of] harm you will change and become a beast; [if you think of] compassion you will change and become a Bodhisattva. [If you think of] intuitive wisdom you will change and enter the upper realms; [if you think of] ignorance you will change and enter the lower quarters. The changes of your own natures are extreme, yet the deluded person is not himself conscious of this. [Successive thoughts give rise to evil and evil ways are always practiced]. But if a single thought of good evolves, intuitive wisdom is born. [This is called the *Nirmānakāya* Buddha of your own nature. What is the perfect *Sambhogakāya* Buddha?] As one lamp serves to dispel a thousand years of darkness, so one flash of wisdom destroys ten thousand years of ignorance. Do no think of the past; always think of the future; if your future thoughts are always good, you may be called the *Sambhogakāya* Buddha. An instant of thought of evil will result in the destruction of good which has continued a thousand years; an instant of thought of good compensates for a thousand years of evil and destruction. If from the timeless beginning future thoughts have always been good, you may be called the *Sambhogakāya* Buddha. Observed from the standpoint of the *Dharmakāya*, this is none ofher than the *Nirmānakāya*. When successive thoughts are good, this then is the *Sambhogakāya*. Self-awakening and self-practice, this is 'to take refuge.' Skin and flesh form the physical body; the physical body is the home. This has nothing to do with taking refuge. If, however, you awaken to the threefold body, then you have understood the cardinal meaning.

"Now that you have already taken refuge in the threefold body of Buddha, I shall expound to you the four great vows. Good friends, recite in unison what I say: 'I vow to save all sentient beings everywhere. I vow to cut off all the passions everywhere. I vow to study all the Buddhist teachings everywhere. I vow to achieve the unsurpassed Buddha Way.' (Recite three times.)

"Good friends, when I say 'I vow to save all sentient beings everywhere,' it is not that I will save you, but that sentient beings, each with their own natures, must save themselves. What is meant by 'saving yourselves with your own natures'? Despite heterodox views, passions, ignorance, and delusions, in your own physical bodies you have in your selves the attributes of inherent enlightenment,[1] so that with correct views you can be saved. If you are awakened to

---

[1] The subtleties of the concept of enlightenment are numerous and confusing. Yampolsky clarifies an important distinction in one of his many helpful notes to this translation: This term is "used in contradistinction to *shih-chüeh*, the initial enlightenment, which is gained by means of practice, and which enables one to awaken to the ultimate reality. Since initial enlightenment exists because of original enlightenment, the two separate terms are used; however, once awakening is gained through practice, the two become the same." Readers interested in a detailed, scholarly study of this sutra should turn to Yampolsky's fine translation published by Columbia University Press, 1967.

correct views, the wisdom of *prajña* will wipe away ignorance and delusion and you will all save yourselves. If false
views come, with correct views you will be saved; if delusion
comes, with awakening you will be saved; if ignorance
comes, with wisdom you will be saved; if evil comes, with
good you will be saved; if the passions come, with *bodhi* you
will be saved. Being saved in this way is known as true
salvation.

" 'I vow to cut off all the passions everywhere' is, with
your own minds to cast aside the unreal and the false. 'I vow
to study all the Buddhist teachings everywhere' is to study
the unsurpassed true Dharma. 'I vow to achieve the unsurpassed Buddha Way' is always to act humbly, to practice
reverence for all things, to separate oneself from erroneous
attachments, and to awaken to the wisdom of *prajña*. When
delusions are cast aside you are self-enlightened, achieve the
Buddha Way, and put into practice the power of the vows.

㊗

The Master said: "Good friends, if you wish to practice,
it is all right to do so as laymen; you don't have to be in a
temple. If you are in a temple but do not practice, you are
like the evil-minded people of the West. If you are a layman
but do practice, you are practicing the good of the people
of the East. Only I beg of you, practice purity yourselves;
this then is the Western Land."

The prefect asked: "Master, how should we practice as
laymen? I wish you would instruct us."

The Master said: "Good friends, I shall make a formless
verse for you monks and laymen. When all of you recite it
and practice according to it, then you will always be in the
same place as I am. The verse says:

Proficiency in preaching and proficiency in the mind,
Are like the sun and empty space.
Handing down this sudden teaching alone,
Enter into the world and destroy erroneous doctrines.
Although in the teaching there is no sudden and gradual,

In delusion and awakening there is slowness and speed.
In studying the teaching of the sudden doctrine,[1]
Ignorant persons cannot understand completely.
Although explanations are made in ten thousand ways,
If you combine them with the principle, they become one.
Within the dark home of the passions,
The sun of wisdom must at all times shine.
Erroneous [thoughts] come because of the passions;
When correct [thoughts] come the passions are cast aside.
Use neither the erroneous nor the correct,
And with purity you will attain to complete Nirvana.
Although enlightenment [*bodhi*] is originally pure,
Creating the mind that seeks it is then delusion.
The pure nature exists in the midst of delusions,
With correct [thoughts] alone remove the three obstacles.[2]
If people in this world practice the Way,
There is nothing whatsoever to hinder them.
If they always make clear the guilt within themselves,
Then they will accord with the Way.
All living thingsof themselves possess the Way;
If you part from the Way and seek it elsewhere,
Seek it you may, but you will not find it,
And in the end, indeed, you will be disappointed.
If you aspire to attain the Way,
Practice correctly; this is the Way.
If in yourselves you do not have the correct mind,
You will be walking in darkness and will not see the Way.
If you are a person who truly practices the Way,
Do not look at the ignorance of the world,
For if you see the wrong of people in the world,
Being wrong yourself, *you* will be evil.
The wrong in others is not your own crime,
Your own wrong is of itself your crime.

---

[1] An alternative translation of this line reads: "In this teaching of seeing into one's own true nature."

[2] The passions, deeds done, and retributions.

Only remove the wrong in your own mind,
Crush the passions and destroy them.
If you wish to convert an ignorant person,
Then you must have expedients.
Do not allow him to have doubts,
Then enlightenment *(bodhi)*[1] will appear.
From the outset the Dharma has been in the world;
Being in the world, it transcends the world.
Hence do not seek the transcendental world outside,
By discarding the present world itself.
Erroneous views are of this world,
Correct views transcend this world.
If you smash completely the erroneous and the correct,
[Then the nature of enlightenment *(bodhi)* will be revealed
   as it is].
Just this is the Sudden Teaching;
Another name for it is the Mahāyāna.
Having been deluded throughout a multitude of kalpas,
One gains awakening within an instant.

卍

"The mind has nothing to do with thinking, because its fundamental source is empty. To discard false views, this is the one great causal event. If within and without you are not deluded then you are apart from duality. If on the outside you are deluded you cling to form; if on the inside you are deluded you cling to emptiness. If within form you are apart from form and within emptiness you are separated from emptiness, then within and without you are not deluded. If you awaken to this Dharma, in one instant of thought your mind will open and you will go forth in the world. What is it that the mind opens? It opens Buddha's wisdom and the Buddha means enlightenment. Separately considered there

[1]Yampolsky notes that another rendering of this line substitutes "self-nature" for "enlightenment *(bodhi)*."

are four gates: the opening of the wisdom of enlightenment, the instruction of the wisdom of enlightenment, the awakening of the wisdom of enlightenment, and the entering into the wisdom of enlightenment. This is called opening, instructing, awakening, and entering.[1] Entering from one place, this is the wisdom of enlightenment, and [with this] you see into your own nature, and succeed in transcending the world."

The Sixth Patriarch said: "Hear me as I explain to you. If men in later generations wish to seek the Buddha, they have only to know that the Buddha mind is within sentient beings; then they will be able to know the Buddha. Because the Buddha mind is possessed by sentient beings, apart from sentient beings there is no Buddha mind.

Deluded, a Buddha is a sentient bieng;
Awakened, a sentient being is a Buddha.
Ignorant, a Buddha is a sentient being;
With wisdom, a sentient being is a Buddha.
If the mind is warped, a Buddha is a sentient bieng;
If the mind is impartial, a sentient being is a Buddha.
When once a warped mind is produced,
Buddha is concealed within the sentient being.
If for one instant of thought we become impartial,
Then sentient beings are themselves Buddha.
In our mind itself a Buddha exists,

[1]The translator draws an important comparison here to the Lotus Sutra, where there is the following passage: "Sariputra, why did the various Buddhas and the World-honored One, just because of the one great causal even, appear in the world? The various Buddhas and the Buddha's wisdom for sentient beings and enable them to become pure. Because they wanted to *instruct* sentient beings in the wisdom of Buddha, they appeared in the world. Because they wanted to bring the *awakening* of Buddha's wisdom to sentient beings, they appeared in the world. Because they wanted to have sentient beings *enter* into the way of Buddha's wisdom, they appeared in the world." Yampolsky points out that the four stages mentioned here correspond to the four gates described in the Sutra.

Our own Buddha is the true Buddha.
If we do not have in ourselves the Buddha mind,
Then where are we to seek Buddha?"

The Master said: "My disciples, farewell. I am going to leave you a verse entitled the 'Self-nature true Buddha emancipation' verse. Should deluded men in later generations grasp the purport of this verse, they will see the true Buddha of their own minds and of their own self-natures. With this verse I shall part from you. The verse says:

True reality and a pure nature—this is the true Buddha;
Evil views and the three poisons—this is the true demon.
For the person with evil views, the demon is in his home;
For the person with correct views, the Buddha will call at
　his home.
If from the evil views within the nature the three poisons
　are produced,
This means that a demon king has come to reside in the
　home.
If correct views of themselves cast aside the mind of the
　three poisons,
The demon changes and becomes a Buddha, one that is
　true, not false.
The *Nirmānakāya*, the *Sambhogakāya*, the *Dharmakāya*,
These three bodies are from the outset one body.
If within your own nature you seek to see for yourself,
This then is the cause of becoming Buddha and gaining
　enlightenment *(bodhi)*.
Since from the outset the *Nirmānakāya* produces the pure
　nature,
This pure nature is always contained within the *Nirmānak
　āya*.
If your nature activates the *Nirmānakāya* to practice the
correct way,
In the future perfection is achieved, a perfection true and
　without limit.
The licentious nature is itself the cause of purity,
Outside of licentiousness there is no pure nature.

If only within your self-nature you yourself separate from the
five desires,
The instant you see into your own nature—this is the True
[Buddha].
If in this life you awaken to the teaching of the Sudden
Doctrine.
Awakening, you will see the World-honored One before
your eyes.
If you wish to practice and say you seek the Buddha,
Who knows where you will find the True [One]?
If within your own body you yourself have the True,
Where the True is, there is the means of becoming Buddha.
If you do not seek the True yourself and seek the Buddha
outside,
All your seeking will be that of a highly ignorant man.
The teaching of the Sudden Doctrine has come from the
West [?].
To save people of the world you must practice yourself.
Now I say to all Ch'an students in this world,
If you do not rely on this Way you are leading vacant lives."

The Master, having finished his verse, then said to his
disciples: "Good-by, all of you. I shall depart from you now.
After I am gone, do not weep wordly tears, nor accept
condolences, money, and silks from people, nor wear mourning garments. If you did so it would not accord with the
sacred Dharma, nor would you be true disciples of mine. Be
the same as you would if I were here, and sit all together in
meditation. If you are only peacefully calm and quiet, with-
out motion, without stillness, without birth, without destruction, without coming, without going, without judgments of right and wrong, without staying and without
going—this then is the Great Way.